ARCEAU LE TEMPS VOYAGEUR

TIME, AN HERMÈS OBJECT.

HERMÈS
PARIS

One plot, one wine, one ingredient.

A cornerstone of Krug's savoir-faire, individuality is the art of understanding that every plot of vines gives birth to a unique wine, itself a single ingredient in Krug Champagnes.

As a tribute to our craftsmanship, each year the House of Krug invites chefs around the world on a culinary journey around a single ingredient and the many pleasures it can reveal when paired with a glass of Krug Grande Cuvée or Krug Rosé.

This year, we celebrate Rice.

KRUG

CHAMPAGNE

HOUSE OF FINN JUHL

The Whisky Chair

The Whisky Chair was designed by Finn Juhl in 1948 and is characterized by the designer's artistic sense of shape, function, and detail. The exclusive chair was originally presented at the Cabinetmakers' Guild Exhibition in 1948, as part of Finn Juhl's concept "The Living Room of an Art Collector", but was not put into production. Finn Juhl always dared to stand alone and was unconcerned about the critics who found his designs too extravagant. Now, the time has finally come for one of the most daring designs to have its revival.

The Whisky Chair's characteristic design includes a half-moon shaped tray in polished brass. The tray unfolds into a full circle where a hole in the brass surface is shaped to hold the accompanying mouth-blown whisky glass.

Fleur

Fleur Collection

COMING SOON
New travel books from *Kinfolk*

Kinfolk Islands marks the start of an exciting new series of titles with
Artisan Books that foster thoughtful perspectives on the places we
visit. Join us on a journey off the beaten track, to islands big and
small, in this collection of 18 new travel stories.

Pre-order now at Kinfolk.com

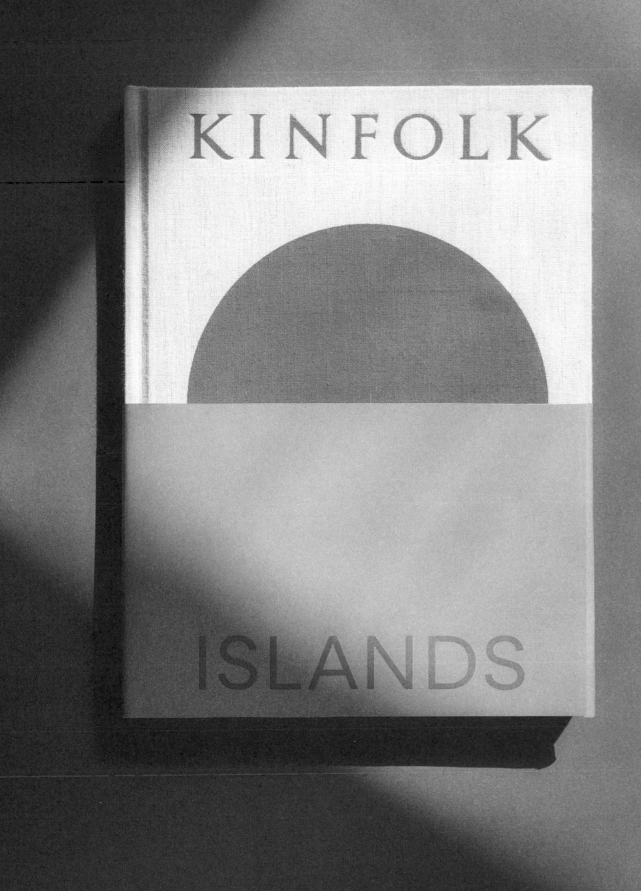

KINFOLK

MAGAZINE
—

EDITOR IN CHIEF	John Burns
EDITOR	Harriet Fitch Little
ART DIRECTOR	Christian Møller Andersen
DESIGN DIRECTOR	Alex Hunting
COPY EDITOR	Rachel Holzman

STUDIO
—

PUBLISHING DIRECTOR	Edward Mannering
STUDIO & PROJECT MANAGER	Susanne Buch Petersen
DESIGNER & ART DIRECTOR	Staffan Sundström
DIGITAL MANAGER	Cecilie Jegsen

—

CROSSWORD	Mark Halpin
PUBLICATION DESIGN	Alex Hunting Studio
COVER PHOTOGRAPH	Romain Laprade

The views expressed in *Kinfolk* magazine are those of the respective contributors and are not necessarily shared by the company or its staff. *Kinfolk* (ISSN 2596-6154) is published quarterly by Ouur ApS, Amagertorv 14B, 2, 1160 Copenhagen, Denmark. Printed by Park Communications Ltd in London, United Kingdom. Color reproduction by Park Communications Ltd in London, United Kingdom. All rights reserved. No part of this publication may be reproduced, distributed or transmitted in any form or by any means, including photocopying or other electronic or mechanical methods, without prior written permission of the editor in chief, except in the case of brief quotations embodied in critical reviews and certain other noncommercial uses permitted by copyright law. The US annual subscription price is $75 USD. Airfreight and mailing in the USA by WN Shipping USA, 156-15, 146th Avenue, 2nd Floor, Jamaica, NY 11434, USA. Application to mail at periodicals postage prices is pending at Jamaica, NY 11431. US Postmaster: Send address changes to *Kinfolk*, WN Shipping USA, 156-15, 146th Avenue, 2nd Floor, Jamaica, NY 11434, USA. Subscription records are maintained at Ouur ApS, Amagertorv 14B, 2, 1160 Copenhagen, Denmark. SUBSCRIBE: *Kinfolk* is published four times a year. To subscribe, visit kinfolk.com/subscribe or email us at info@kinfolk.com. CONTACT US: If you have questions or comments, please write to us at info@kinfolk.com. For advertising and partnership inquiries, get in touch at advertising@kinfolk.com.

WORDS
—

Precious Adesina
Annabel Bai Jackson
Nana Biamah-Ofosu
Malaika Byng
Rachel Connolly
Ed Cumming
Stephanie d'Arc Taylor
Daphnée Denis
Tom Faber
Harriet Fitch Little
Robert Ito
Rosalind Jana
Janis Jefferies
Nathan Ma
Jenna Mahale
Okechukwu Nzelu
Hettie O'Brien
Sala Elise Patterson
Debika Ray
Asher Ross
Laura Rysman
Kabelo Sandile Motsoeneng
Charles Shafaieh
Doree Shafrir
Selena Takigawa Hoy
George Upton
Alice Vincent
Tom Whyman

STYLING, SET DESIGN, HAIR & MAKEUP
—

Nika Ambrožic
Poppy Buntz
Elisa Clark
Kelsey James
Camilla Larsson
Jinny Kim
Bjorn Krischker
Jèss Monterde
James O'Riley
Giulia Querenghi
Stephanie Stamatis
Holly White

ARTWORK & PHOTOGRAPHY
—

Lauren Bamford
Ted Belton
Henrik Bülow
Scottie Cameron
Justin Chung
Pelle Crépin
Thomas Cristiani
Marina Denisova
Adrien Dirand
Lara Downie
Yuji Fukuhara
Richard Gaston
Felicity Ingram
Cecilie Jegsen
Romain Laprade
Alixe Lay
Lola + Pani
Matzo & Matzo
Constantin Mirbach
Pierrot
Rick Pushinsky
Gerd Rothmann
Paul Rousteau
Josefine Seifert
Julian Song
Lisa Sorgini
Monica Steffensen
Staffan Sundström
Adrien Toubiana
Minh Tran
Emma Trim
Andrea Urbez

PUBLISHER
—

Chul-Joon Park

VIPP

V1 Kitchen

The chef's home office

Our modular kitchen is built to be used.
Nothing but stainless steel, powder-coated
endurance and a workstation made for
the most demanding guests.

VIPP.COM

WELCOME
The Great Outdoors

In crime theory, there is a principle that every contact leaves a trace. The same is true of our relationship with nature; however hard you try to cover your tracks, the mud, pollen and spores that cling to you would allow a forensic botanist to retrace your path with a high degree of accuracy. Even your mood might give the game away; studies have shown that walking in deciduous forests can significantly lower your blood pressure.

The same principle applies the other way around. Every human engagement with the great outdoors will leave its mark, whether that's one twig broken underfoot or a butterfly effect set in motion whenever people cut down forests, divert rivers or wipe out biodiversity by planting a new, huge monocrop.

Each person we interview in The Great Outdoors section of this issue is thinking about how to mediate these contact moments in fresh and nuanced ways. In Scotland, we meet Thomas Mac-Donell, the conservationist whose mission to "rewild" the Highlands means understanding the chain of human-led events that made the landscape so barren in the first place. In Japan, we spend the day with Snow Peak president Lisa Yamai, who explains how to make outdoor gear that eases the friction between vulnerable bodies and extreme weather conditions. In the US, archaeologist Ayana Omilade Flewellen talks about their hunt for the physical traces that humans leave behind in nature; they spend their days diving for the remnants of slave ships, recovering human histories buried in the deep. For everyone we speak to—from garden designer Piet Oudolf to explorer Ella Al-Shamahi—the sense of responsibility is countered by an extreme joy in nature that led them to pursue a career outdoors in the first place. As Flewellen puts it, "The great outdoors for me feels like freedom, the great escape."

We hope the issue inspires you to step outside and see your surroundings anew. If you prefer to stay curled up at home, then the rest of the issue will provide you with comfort—and company. We're hugely excited to be featuring someone who many readers will feel they already know intimately—yoga instructor Adriene Mishler. In London, Zawe Ashton talks about wanting to become a writer even as her acting career is going stratospheric, and in Paris, the owners of Galerie Chenel invite us inside their astonishing, antiques-filled apartment. There are short interviews with two up-and-coming designers, Mac Collins and Bianca Saunders, plus a conversation with artists Gerard & Kelly about how choreography and performance art can help us reexamine the legacies of modernist architects.

WORDS
JOHN BURNS
HARRIET FITCH LITTLE

Calum Lounge — Comfort
design Simon Pengelly
2022

www.desalto.it

DESALTO

ph Andrea Ferrari

Fiorini trading (Scandinavian countries)
Ph +45 20683808 — info@fiorinitrading.dk

STARTERS
A serving of smart ideas.

FEATURES
Islands, interiors and internet fame.

"I have a terrible habit of wearing my heart on my sleeve." (Adriene Mishler – P. 53)

CESAR

Portraits of me.

Kitchen: **Unit**
Design: **García Cumini**

Milano • New York • Paris

cesar.it

CONTENTS

THE GREAT OUTDOORS
Step outside and rewild your world.

DIRECTORY
Culture, columns and a crossword.

Photograph: Richard Gaston

STARTERS:

LOVE THAT FOR YOU
A lesson in the art of compersion.

Do you think of happiness as a limited resource? That is arguably the implicit, if illogical, feeling underlying emotions like jealousy, envy and schadenfreude—that one person's luck comes at the expense of your own.

An envious worldview frames the positive stuff in life as a finite pool that can be depleted, much like money, which capitalism has bound tightly to notions of satisfaction. When you see someone else's good fortune through jealous eyes, you want it too; when they suffer, you might feel they have been brought down closer to your level. This scarcity mindset can make it difficult to be happy for a friend when they are offered a new job, jet off on vacation or land a gorgeous new partner.

Of course, happiness is not the same as money: There should be more than enough to go around. The polyamorous community, famed for having liberal and progressive attitudes toward love, sex and relationships, understands this more than most. It's possible to be happy even when the person who lands a hot new lover is your own partner. There is even a word for it: compersion.[1]

"It's the feeling of secondhand pleasure at an intimate partner's enjoyment elsewhere—a fancy word for 'happy for you,'" one anonymous non-monogamist tells me. My interviewee suggests that if you can apply this principle in your intimate relationships it may also give you the skills to enjoy the rest of your life more: Practice avoiding FOMO by feeling genuinely happy for other people when they succeed or enjoy themselves.

It's an idea that is also being considered by *Archives of Sexual Behavior*, the official publication of the International Academy of Sex Research, which published a paper last year about a new tool to measure compersion. Next, its authors plan to research whether and how this feeling can be nurtured and developed to help loosen the grip of jealousy more generally.

But for even the most enlightened, compersion can be a difficult emotion to access. It's for the same reasons—personal insecurity, negative comparison with others and the fear of losing someone or something—that envy and jealousy exist in the wider world. Our daily interactions with friends and strangers have always been complicated by emotional baggage, but such experiences can seem more acute in an era when we're continuously exposed to a filtered and airbrushed version of other people's lives online. In contrast, our own existence can often feel like an arduous and isolating uphill climb. How, then, can one possibly feel "happy for you"?

In polyamory—as in all life—there are no easy solutions, my adviser says. You can only work hard to cultivate better communication, openness, patience with yourself and gratitude for what you have: "If you can find ways to believe your own situation is good enough and make it so, both materially and psychologically, then you can experience compersion in a wider sense."

WORDS
DEBIKA RAY
PHOTO
STAFFAN SUNDSTRÖM

(1) The term "compersion" was coined by a member of the Kerista Commune, a utopian community in San Francisco that made money selling Macintosh computers in the 1980s. At one point, they were the largest Macintosh dealership in Northern California. The computers were also used to draw up the schedule of whom would copulate with whom on any given night.

THE PREMONITIONS BUREAU

WORDS
GEORGE UPTON
PHOTO
ADRIEN TOUBIANA
& THOMAS CRISTIANI

Four questions about foreboding feelings.

Sam Knight's book *The Premonitions Bureau* explores the phenomenon of premonitions through the gripping account of a British experiment run in the late 1960s. For 18 months, psychiatrist John Barker and the *Evening Standard*'s science correspondent, Peter Fairley, operated the Premonitions Bureau, collecting premonitions from the newspaper's readers and publishing those that appeared to come true. Here, Knight explains how the Bureau's research blurred the line between science and the supernatural, and how the phenomenon of premonitions can reveal something fundamental about the way we see and interpret the world around us today.

GEORGE UPTON: What is a premonition?

SAM KNIGHT: The definition I find most useful is that it's not just a hunch or an intuition, which anyone might have experienced, but something that you know for a fact will happen. It presents you with a dilemma: Do you act on it or try to forget about it?

GU: When did researchers start to become interested in premonitions as a phenomenon?

SK: The thinking around the paranormal and parapsychology really hit its peak around the turn of the century and the First World War, when there was this combination of technical progress and anxiety. What makes the Premonitions Bureau interesting is that it came at a time of rampant scientific advances. It's really telling to me that Fairley is flying out to watch preparations for the Apollo mission and then coming back to his office at the *Evening Standard* and riffling through the latest predictions sent into the Bureau. There's this vertiginous feeling of progress in all directions and a sense that we should also expand our understanding of what the human mind is capable of.

GU: How was the experiment received at the time?

SK: It was not a rigorous peer-reviewed scientific experiment. Of the 469 predictions that came in the first year, 18 were reported by Fairley to be hits. You could think of that 3% success rate as proving that there's something there, or that it's all hokum. There was a real backlash to the Bureau's approach in the 1970s. Most of the parapsychological research institutions were shut down and there's a consensus that as well as not being very scientific, it was not particularly healthy. So, that was really the moment where you start to have the strict bifurcation between science and the supernatural that has become the status quo today.

GU: What can we learn more broadly about human nature from the Bureau's research?

SK: One of the things I draw out of it is how we seem to be wired to make predictions. There's a recent idea in neuroscience called the predictive brain, which suggests that we are already relying on our memories and our knowledge to infer what's going to happen next. Premonitions are only one step beyond this natural and universal process, but it tends not to be a very fruitful way of thinking. There's a really nice Arthur Koestler quote in the book about how experiencing these coincidences can be "as if some mute power were tugging at your sleeve," but it's up to you whether you do anything with it.

WORDS
TOM WHYMAN
PHOTO
LISA SORGINI

Michel de Montaigne, the 16th-century French writer, tells us in one of his *Essays* that we cannot be deemed happy until after we die, because how we die might void any or all of the happiness we experienced in life. A great king might be executed by one of his rivals, after having his lands seized and all of his heirs killed. By contrast, an "execrable and ill-famed" man might leave this mortal coil "in all respects perfectly reconciled" to those around him.

If we can only "really" understand a life after it is over, we are apparently doomed never to understand our own. Any insight we might at some point gain into ourselves is only temporary; standing always to be revised. Examples from literature might seem to bear this point out. Most novels don't bother trying to describe the entire sweep of the lives of their protagonists, from birth to death. But those that do—think Bruce Chatwin's rural tragedy of frustrated hopes *On the Black Hill*, or John le Carré's semi-autobiographical *A Perfect Spy*—are typically compelled to start not with the moment of their central character's birth, but rather with the story of how they were conceived.

Lives overrun their own confines: The titular narrator in Laurence Sterne's *Tristram Shandy* expends two full volumes before even managing to get to his birth, while the story of troubled young artist Duncan Thaw that Alasdair Gray tells in *Lanark* starts with his afterlife, only later working back to his death.

The problem, it seems, is getting the right sort of perspective: the right vista, from which to see what matters about a life as a whole. This is where Chatwin, for one, succeeds. Toward the end of *On the Black Hill*, there is a moment where the elderly Lewis, one of the twin farmers the book has focused on—a character who has spent his whole life longing for, and being denied, adventure—finally gets to ride in an airplane. "And suddenly he felt," Chatwin writes, "that all the frustrations of his cramped and frugal life now counted for nothing, because, for ten magnificent minutes, he had done what he wanted to do." And so Lewis is allowed to die happy. At the book's end, his sad, small life has been redeemed.

THE WHOLE STORY
The power of cradle-to-grave novels.

Sometimes we flag the obviousness of what we're about to say to avoid seeming condescending or clueless. In January 2021, facing criticism over the COVID-19 vaccine rollout, Dr. Anthony Fauci said in an interview on the *Today* show, "Obviously, we have to do better than that." He stated that he was stating the obvious—because not doing so would make him appear out of touch with public opinion.

Sometimes, though, using the codicil "obvious" is meant to shame the listener: You haven't read the memo, you are deficient in common sense. Indeed, the shame attached to missing the obvious—or to stating what is obvious while under the impression that it is not—runs deep. Nothing is worse than offering a brilliant suggestion, only to realize that many heads have already nodded it into action: The point has already been made, the proposal is in place. At such times, we might preemptively announce that we are "stating the obvious" not merely to indicate that

we have been listening, but also to spare our blushes. Stating the obvious is a rhetorical device, so it is unsurprising that what lies beneath is rather complicated. What is obvious, and to whom? On what commonalities do "shared understandings" depend? In Brit Bennett's 2020 novel, *The Vanishing Half*, the severe social unrest following the assassination of Martin Luther King Jr. alarms the white Los Angeles neighborhood of Palace Estates—less so for resident Stella Vignes, who has been passing for white, and whose Black father was lynched in front of her when she was a child: "The country was unrecognizable now, [her neighbor] Cath Johansen said, but it looked the same as it ever had to Stella." Perhaps there is some shame attached to being one of many heads nodding in the same direction, never needing to look across at those who have long been clamoring for change. When our shared understandings evolve, this can only be a good thing—surely that's obvious.

WORDS
OKECHUKWU NZELU
PHOTO
FELICITY INGRAM

BASIC INSTINCTS
The importance of being obvious.

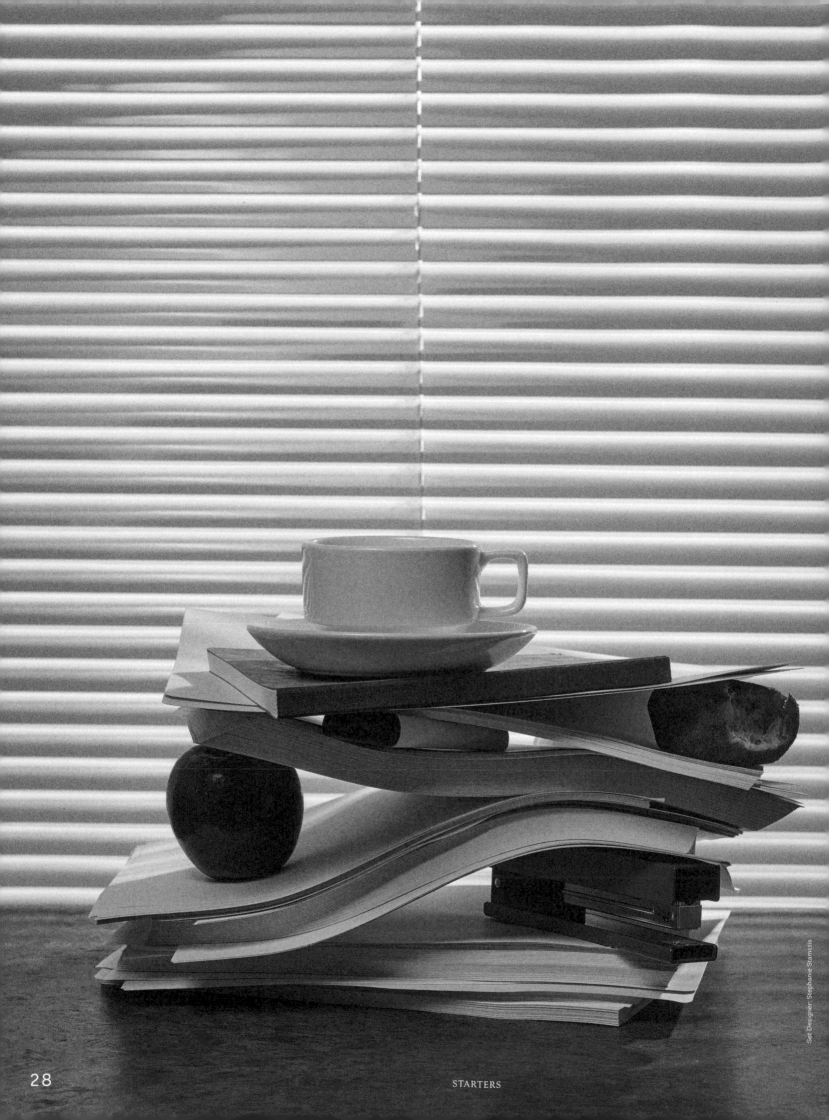

Recently, the literary world has embraced the "literary privilege disclaimer." The concept, first detailed by Emma Specter in *Vogue*, consists of a few lines—or a few pages—in which a writer explains that they understand their privilege and power in society and how it translates to their work.[1] Ultimately, the literary privilege disclaimer is an author's shield against the public's ethical concerns about what it means to write outside of one's experience and who gets to be celebrated for such an attempt. It inoculates the writer from criticism if their identity contradicts the experiences documented in their work.

The inclusion of the disclaimer does not change the content but it shapes how the reader might receive the work. It trains the reader to focus their gaze and attention on the author, to detect the ways in which the author is trying their best not to offend. It also protects the author and their publisher from backlash that might harm sales. Imagine if the polarizing *A Little Life* by Hanya Yanagihara had contained a privilege statement explaining that while the story about an abused gay man living with a physical disability was a long way from the author's own experiences as an upper-middle-class woman, she felt it worth telling. Yanagihara would have protected herself from some of the indignation that followed.

The literary disclaimer is a product of its identity-obsessed time. We live in a time where the author is not dead; in fact, we often rely on their biography to engage with their work. Yet all these moves are a distraction from what we can gain from art: to be surprised and moved by beauty. Legal disclaimers exist for a reason—they protect all parties involved, especially on issues of copyright. The case for the literary privilege disclaimer, however, is unconvincing: Does it indicate that the writer is honest and wants to put all their cards on the table? Does it mean that readers and critics have to forgive a writer who failed to produce an honest, complex and moving narrative and instead leaned toward the shallow and reductive? It is clear why this disclaimer exists: It protects an anxious industry from scrutiny, but it also alters how we publicly engage with literature.

(1) In her article for *Vogue*, Specter interviews publishing agent Angeline Rodriguez who offers the following critique: "If your acknowledgment of your privilege isn't already baked into what you're saying, then I don't know that tacking it on in order to head off Twitter criticism or what have you is beneficial to the reader."

WORDS
KABELO SANDILE MOTSOENENG
PHOTO
LAUREN BAMFORD

OPEN BOOKS
Introducing the literary privilege disclaimer.

SHOW YOUR CARDS

WORDS
NATHAN MA
PHOTO
MONICA STEFFENSEN

Advice from a greeting card expert.

By now, a "Hallmark moment" is much more than a slogan. The phrase has become shorthand for a pitch-perfect memory made between two people, the kind that can be commemorated with a greeting card. Courtney Taylor knows this feeling well. "Cards have always occupied a very big part of my life and childhood," she explains, speaking from her home in Kansas City, Missouri. Although you likely don't know Taylor by name, you've probably seen her work: As a writer at Hallmark, her words can be found on mugs, on social media posts for Mahogany (the company's collection celebrating Black culture), in viral videos and, yes, on greeting cards too. Here, Taylor shares the secrets to writing a great card.

NATHAN MA: What makes a memorable greeting card?

COURTNEY TAYLOR: A memorable card is a mirror that reflects a valuable emotion or belief back to you. It's seeing yourself in the words and the art that's depicted—it's feeling like the card is yours even though it was written entirely by somebody else that you don't know.

NM: As a card writer, how do you tap into feelings and relationships that are often quite specific?

CT: Sometimes we have projects about certain topics like cards that you send to someone with whom you don't have a good relationship: How do you say, "I still love you no matter what our relationship is like," and keep it uplifting? That's a big part: We never really want to end it on a bad note. It always has to come back to a hopeful place.

NM: Are there any briefs that you remember fondly?

CT: For one of my favorite cards, I received the concept for the imagery first. They wanted to do a parody for Mahogany: "The 12 Do's of Christmas." Another writer and I came up with the lyrics to the song: "11 festive fades, 10 faux locs, 9 cornrows . . ." It's a really cute card, and it has all the hairstyles on the cover.

NM: When it comes to writing a personal message in a greeting card, what are the dos?

CT: Lean into your voice, and use the card in whatever way necessary to make sure your message is coming through. It might help to think about what you want to say before you take out the pen, or maybe you want it to be a stream of consciousness—an organic outpouring from the heart. Lean into vulnerability and candor.

NM: And what are the don'ts?

CT: Don't force it. It's okay to just sign your name and send the card. See writing a note as an opportunity to start a conversation—the intent of a greeting card is to open an emotional door. How you open that door, the language you use, the color of the pen you use, all of that is up to you.

NM: There are plenty of obvious opportunities to send a greeting card: birthdays, anniversaries, condolences, holidays. What opportunities do most people overlook?

CT: The "just because" card that you send just because someone's on your mind. We often forget that we don't need a reason to celebrate others, and that life itself is an occasion worth acknowledging every day.

32

WORD: EXPLICATION
An explanation to end all explanations.

Etymology: No, it isn't French for "explanation." Instead, the word "explication" refers to a cognitive method used by analytical philosophers and scientists. It was most famously defined by German-born American philosopher Rudolf Carnap in 1950 as a way to transform "an inexact prescientific concept, the explicandum, into a new exact concept, the explicatum." In that sense, explicating goes beyond explaining. An explication has the power to change the way we understand the world by replacing a lack of data—or vague, incorrect notions—with scientifically proven facts.

Meaning: An event that has been widely accepted as an explication is when, in 2006, the International Astronomical Union (IAU) published a definition of "planet." Until then, nine bodies orbiting around the sun had been recognized as such, but there were no clear guidelines as to what the definitive characteristics of a planet should be. After several objects other than the original nine were discovered orbiting, the IAU had to clarify this important astronomical matter. A planet, the organization announced, is "a celestial body that (a) is in orbit around the Sun, (b) has sufficient mass for its self-gravity to overcome rigid body forces so that it assumes a hydrostatic equilibrium (nearly round) shape, and (c) has cleared the neighbourhood around its orbit." This effectively meant Pluto was demoted and no longer qualified as a planet. A formerly imprecise concept was replaced by an accurate one, changing our perception of the world and the skies.

Explication underpins modern evolution: It's how humans trade beliefs for empirically backed conclusions. It's how science and technology unveil the unknown, sometimes with overwhelming consequences.[1] German thinker Peter Sloterdijk considers explication to be a frightening process. "When the implicit becomes explicit," Sloterdijk writes, "something completely willful, foreign, different, something never intended, never expected, and never to be assimilated penetrates thought."

The more we know about how the world works, the more vulnerable we may feel. Explicating how global warming will impact the world in the years to come empowers us with understanding while also making us feel helpless. Radioactivity, carbon emissions, DNA, and even how our galaxies work will always feel extraneous and foreign. In that sense, explication may bring the world forward through science and technology, but it also makes it feel increasingly remote from humans.

WORDS
DAPHNÉE DENIS
PHOTO
PAUL ROUSTEAU

(1) Writing in *The Guardian*, essayist Will Rees uses the concept of explication in relation to his acquiring a huge amount of knowledge about the human body in order to diagnose a mysterious illness he is suffering from. "On the one hand, this increases our technical mastery over the environment; on the other, it brings a sense of vulnerability. There are so many ways that something complicated can go wrong," he writes.

GERARD & KELLY

WORDS
CHARLES SHAFAIEH
PHOTOS
ADRIEN DIRAND

On dance, domesticity and the giants of modernism.

From Philip Johnson's Glass House to Mies van der Rohe's Edith Farnsworth House, many iconic modernist homes have now become what American artists Gerard & Kelly call "ruins." Their transgressive and often utopic ideals either forgotten or intentionally ignored, these sites often lie empty or, transformed into museums, welcome visitors into their fossilized interiors. In Brennan Gerard and Ryan Kelly's ongoing film and performance project *Modern Living*, the Paris-based duo revivifies these structures through a lush, humorous and energetic fusion of movement, words and music.[1]

Their most recent film, *Bright Hours*, turns Cité Radieuse, Le Corbusier's experimental Marseille housing complex, into the transatlantic ocean liner on which he and performer Josephine Baker had a romance. The architect, played by actress Jeanne Balibar, dances joyously to original music by Moses Sumney. As this playful piece suggests, Gerard & Kelly are not interested in a simplistic homage to the modernist project. Rather, they prompt questions about sexual, racial and ethical issues embedded in these strange sites. Their work asks us to consider anew the intimacies and relationships that architecture creates or prohibits.

CHARLES SHAFAIEH: Why is your extended project entitled *Modern Living*?

RYAN KELLY: With an emphasis on movement and dance, we're investigating the form of the couple: its limitations, possibilities, deviations and norms. We started looking back to the historical avant-garde because the contemporary moment can feel so impoverished in terms of big thinking and utopian urges. *Modern Living* is about those relationships that were struggling to modernize in the 1920s and '30s, and how those can be models for all of us as we try to reinvent our most intimate relationships.

BRENNAN GERARD: We started the project at the Schindler House, a two-couple commune in West Hollywood. We took the angle that these relationships were struggling to modernize and they needed new spaces in which that could unfold. That's the "living" part of it.

CS: How do these particular homes—or all homes—produce certain intimacies and relations?

BG: There's a kind of queer claiming of some public spaces—bars, restrooms, parks—whereas the home is thought of as prohibitive of queer life and subjectivity, because often one has to leave the home in order to become queer. We thought about an alternative, utopian history in which the home was a place where queer children were made, and we realized that the modernist architects were often living in proto-queer living arrangements. They didn't have clients; no one wanted their stuff. So they had to produce their own houses first.

RK: The Schindler House collapsed [as a commune] once they started to have children but somehow still seems the most livable space. The Glass House, despite being inhabited by a gay male couple, was for us more complicated. The specter of the closet was really strong, ironically, given its transparency. But we tried to understand how, at a certain moment in history, that kind of closeted culture was maybe productive. The Edith

Farnsworth House was so transgressive that the media had to paint Edith Farnsworth as a kind of communist because it was impossible to comprehend why a woman in her 50s, who was a doctor and poet, would choose to live by herself in a glass house. And then the little-known fact of Le Corbusier and Josephine Baker's relationship. It was wild to speculate how Baker—a woman of color, a dancer, an American—might have impacted his vision of the world, and to think of her alongside Picasso and other modernists.

CS: Are you trying to reintroduce the erotic into these spaces?

RK: Right now I have Rihanna's lyrics "We found love in a hopeless place" in my ears, which is sometimes our agenda! Invention and innovation come from desire.

BG: Sex has been confined to the domestic sphere by capitalism, patriarchy, and heteronormativity. During the performances, we take a once-private space and make it public by bringing the audience inside. It's extremely palpable for the audience because they're very close to the performers.

CS: How does this project resonate with your own homes, past or present?

RK: Where your question lands for me is about the homes that Brennan and I have shared and how our own relationship has evolved and shifted, from romantic partners to post-romantic partners. And throughout that, navigating how to work together, and what friendship and partnership are. In some ways, we're still looking for that designed space that could function as our home and that could support a relationship which is definitely atypical in almost every sense: It's not reproductive but incredibly productive, not romantic but certainly intimate, and involves many long-term and short-term figures passing through it. If the world had an answer to that, we wouldn't have set out to make *Modern Living*.

CS: Are you conscious of how the themes you explore in your art appear in your lives?

RK: People ask us, "Where did the creativity come from? Your family?" I always say, "No." We're two generations from farmers and coal miners. But after my grandmother died last year at 98, my mother was remembering my grandmother's stories about her Italian brothers and sisters, about her family of 13 who played music together and told jokes. And I thought, "Wait a second. That's it. People getting together in a space, making music, moving, making each other laugh." It's very basic and it still courses through [me]. There is some root there.

CS: *Modern Living* notably rejects calls to "cancel" buildings or their architects, regardless of their pasts: Philip Johnson's fascist views, for example. That retort is practically taboo today.

RK: We believe in history. Johnson, van der Rohe—these are not easy people to love. But they're not unlovable. It can be productive to get into bed with them. We lose so much if we just walk away from the mess and violence of history. If we keep pressing the logic of identity politics and cancel culture, and believing that we can simply draw a line in the sand and remake the world, we're going to reach our limit really soon. What's more interesting is to re-narrate these histories, to tell stories differently and find ourselves in them.

BG: In *Bright Hours*, Jeanne Balibar plays Le Corbusier. We don't make a big deal of that. It's the only way it makes sense for us. It's about transforming historical objects for the present moment. It's never just a historical object. In these sites' preservation, there's a tendency that they become dead again and their strangeness is removed. There's an ethics to preserving their strangeness—to accepting that every place and every person is absolutely foreign, including ourselves, at any given moment. We view the performances and the films as kind of alternative forms of presentation and preservation. We're in a moment of moral turpitude in which it's nuanced to return to the radicality of these social experiments—at the Glass House, at the Cité Radieuse—as a way of insisting upon the radicality of difference. Of our relations to each other, and to ourselves. That radical unknowing is very much not the Enlightenment project of categorizing in order to know.

---

(1) Gerard & Kelly often choreograph dance performances around significant buildings or sculptures. In 2018, they worked with Solange Knowles on *Metatronia (Metatron's Cube)*, a film that features a group of dancers moving around a striking white cube sculpture designed by Knowles.

Brennan Gerard (left) and Ryan Kelly (right) were photographed at the Carré d'Art—Musée d'Art Contemporain in Nîmes, France.

WORDS
ED CUMMING
ARTWORK
GERD ROTHMANN

I remember a conversation with a friend, many years ago, in which he described an event as having been "total shausse." Baffled, the others at the table asked him to repeat it. He said it again. "Total shausse." At last the penny dropped. This was an intelligent guy, but he had never said the word "chaos" out loud before.

English is full of words you see written down more often than you hear spoken, and the language is a haven of eccentric pronunciation. As a native speaker, you might think the differences between though, through, thorough, bough and rough are obvious. They are not. Partly the problems stem from English's greed for assimilating other languages, but its erratic approach to anglicization. There is no rule for guiding you through canapé, debacle, apropos, imbroglio, milieu, cache, segue, décolletage, tinnitus, chimera or rigmarole.

Some words are famously difficult but mercifully rare: Few people will attempt synecdoche without a few weeks of training. Other ones have a habit of popping up when you least expect them. These are the real dangers: hyperbole, epitome, anaesthetist. Foodstuffs are a minefield: açai, arugula, hors d'oeuvre, almond, as are certain brand names, not just Nike and Porsche. Our college email system was named for the Greek messenger god, Hermes; pity the glamorous friend who pronounced it like the luxury goods house, Hermès, for two terms.

Although every language has its eccentricities, British English seems particularly culpable. Some American modifications, like ignoring the "h" in "herb," are curious, but overall the pronunciations make more sense, as do their new spellings.

Inevitably, given their silly rules about cutlery, clothing and conversation, the British aristocracy laid down a lot of baffling pronunciation. Sometimes the emphasis is surprising, as in Worcestershire. Elsewhere the language is outright obtuse. Magdalene and Magdalen are both pronounced the same, but not how they ought to be. Were it not for the success of the *Harry Potter* novels, we would still think Hermione might be Hermie-won, or Hermie-own. My own weakness is insouciant. Is it in-SWEE-sunt? Or in-SUE-sea-ont? And I have more or less given up on dachshunds. The mercy, for those of us who find ourselves mispronouncing common words, is that it is not necessarily a sign of stupidity. It might be a sign you are a keen reader, if your written vocabulary greatly exceeds your spoken repertoire. Something to tell your friends, as they wipe the tears of laughter away and face your wrath. Now, is that pronounced "roth" or "rath"?

WORDS UNHEARD
On the pitfalls of pronunciation.

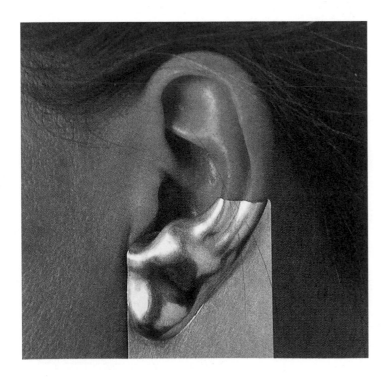

"I got a promise I will not be going to jail." So began comedian Trevor Noah's set at the 2022 White House Correspondents' Dinner, the Washington equivalent of a comedy "roast." With his impunity assured, Noah's job that night was to continue a long-standing tradition of the yearly gala: to publicly mock the president of the United States.

Noah may not have realized it, but his set—with its lighthearted jabs at President Biden's stalled agenda—tapped into a ritual that long precedes today's high-society dinners. In medieval and Renaissance courts, it was the role of the jester to mock the king and his noblemen and elicit their laughter. The concept of "jester's privilege" protected his right to ridicule without facing the chopping block—within reason.

Jester's privilege, after all, was no apolitical gift granted by munificent leaders: It was a way of upholding their power. The custom fashioned a legitimized space to invert the social hierarchy, creating a pressure valve for popular discontent. And the commoners, satiated by their stint of rebellious good humor, would then return to quiescence. The Russian theorist Mikhail Bakhtin developed a framework for understanding these moments of social inversion, which he characterized as "carnivalesque." Bakhtin saw it as a form that was full of subversive potential; for his critics, it was simply blowing off steam.

The principle has been passed down from royal courts to awards ceremonies and celebrity roasts. The cost to the target of mockery? A few excruciating camera cuts that capture their pearly-toothed reaction. And the benefit? A reminder to the public that they, too, can take a joke—that they are self-aware, human, *just like us*.

Now that politicians double as celebrities, embracing jester's privilege can be a smart PR move. Clips of Donald Trump letting Jimmy Fallon tousle his hair, or of Hillary Clinton caricaturing herself on *Saturday Night Live*, promise a welcome boost in virality in a way committee meetings and policy announcements do not. The privilege has continued into the 21st century precisely because it performs a 21st century function: quenching the public's desire for an off-the-books, out-of-hours authenticity. At the end of his set, Noah dutifully reminded the audience what a "blessing" it was, to "speak truth, even if it makes the people in power uncomfortable." Having paid the jester their dues for the year, one imagines that the people in power will carry on just fine.

WORDS
ANNABEL BAI JACKSON
PHOTO
HENRIK BÜLOW

Stylist: Camilla Larsson.

JESTER'S PRIVILEGE
A short history of the comedy roast.

BIANCA SAUNDERS

WORDS
JENNA MAHALE
PHOTO
LOLA + PANI

The future (of menswear) is female.

At least for the moment, Bianca Saunders thinks her favorite color might be electric blue. "And a burnt orange. I love colors that are slightly uneven," she adds, her voice echoing off the bare walls of her studio. The two shades have been a running thread through the SS23 collection the fashion designer is currently formulating. "The new season is all about things being hard and soft," Saunders reveals. "It's brighter than others as well. But I don't want to say too much."

GQ has declared that the 28-year-old London-born designer is "changing the way men dress" with her surreal, sculptural clothes: elegant pieces that transcend the confines of binary gender, and made her a finalist for the LVMH Prize in 2021. Talking through her personal style, formative websites and least favorite fabrics, the designer offers a window into the multidisciplinary future of her brand.

JENNA MAHALE: How do you think the years spent establishing such a fluid brand have impacted your own style?

BIANCA SAUNDERS: It's interesting, actually. I feel like I'm much more on the masculine side of things during the daytime, and then at night it's highly feminine. So I end up wearing more of my brand in the day than at night. I consider myself more in the collections now too; I try on things all the time to see how they look. Because if women do decide to wear my brand, of course it won't look exactly how it does on the men wearing it on the runway. But I think that makes it interesting. It influences how I design too, because the clothes move in slightly different ways.

JM: Are there any materials that you can't stand to work with?

BS: I find Lycra-based fabric a bit difficult. The technical fabrics are a little bit too *technical* for me. But who knows? Maybe next season. When I first started designing, I never thought I'd be using textiles because I didn't like them at all. Knitwear was also something I struggled with, and that's ended up being one of my main interests these past couple of seasons.

JM: You've said before that your view of masculinity was informed in part by your coming of age in digital spaces. What does that mean?

BS: I've always been an internet-based person. Any sort of social media, I was on it. But in my early days, Tumblr was a really good place for me. And I would go on those free download mixtape websites religiously, all the time. Music is a massive influence for me. When I'm starting a collection, I always think about the type of music that I would like in the show. It's never an afterthought, it's always aligned with what I'm working on.

JM: What music have you been drawn to recently?

BS: I've been listening to Kendrick Lamar's new album, a lot of J Dilla as well. And since watching the Kanye West documentary, I've been getting into a lot of his older stuff too.

JM: You've done some exhibition curation before. Is that something that you might return to?

BS: Yeah, definitely! The reason I started my own brand was to have the freedom of creating my worlds in different ways. At the moment, I'm focusing on developing the clothing brand, but I think eventually we'll be making books and exhibitions, supporting friends and artists. This year I've moved into directing my own films—I actually made the AW22 film for the show. It's just about finding the space and time to continue to grow.

THE GIVING TREE
A short history of tree hugging.

STARTERS

The term "tree hugger" evokes a simpler time, one long before there was a consensus that climate change posed an existential threat to humanity, when caring about the environment largely seemed to be the preserve of a small group of activists. In popular culture, tree huggers are usually well-meaning, a little eccentric and easily dismissed as hippies.

But public imagination is fickle; history is much more violent. The original tree huggers were the people of Khejarli, a village in modern-day Rajasthan in India. In 1730, the Maharaja Abhai Singh gave an order to cut down trees in the village for the construction of a new palace. The villagers, for whom the trees were sacred, hugged them to prevent the soldiers from felling them. It was a massacre. After 363 people were killed, Abhai Singh eventually relented.

International summits and celebrity-fronted documentaries may have replaced tree-hugging as a form of protest in recent years, but the practice has since found a new and enthusiastic following in the wellness community. There is now a Tree-Hugging World Championships held in Finland each year (competitors are scored on style and technique).

Studies have shown that hugging a tree can have significant benefits for your health and well-being: Wrapping your arms around a trunk can cause the body to release oxytocin, the hormone associated with feelings of love and intimacy, which reduces stress and anxiety and lowers blood pressure. It might feel a little strange at first, but what's the harm in branching out a little?

—

WORDS
GEORGE UPTON

Left Photograph: Minh Tran. Right Photograph: Matzo & Matzo.

MAC COLLINS

WORDS
NANA BIAMAH-OFOSU
PHOTO
ANDREA URBEZ

Four questions for an emerging designer.

Mac Collins is a young designer whose work is characterized by strong narratives and a rich material culture. Based in the north of England, he is the first recipient of the Ralph Saltzman Prize awarded by the Design Museum in London. His furniture pieces, most notably the Iklwa chair, are bold, intuitive and a joyful celebration of typically peripheral stories.

NANA BIAMAH-OFOSU: Your research at Harewood House in West Yorkshire earlier this year explored the relationship between objects, furniture, Empire and transatlantic slavery. Can you tell us about this project?

MAC COLLINS: The house has a difficult history which, while not hidden, is not entirely visible. I was interested in the Chippendale mahogany furniture collection in the games room which was made from timber sourced from woodlands that were felled to clear land for plantations in 18th-century Jamaica. The piece that I made at Harewood House—a table for playing dominoes, a game that is now synonymous with British Caribbean culture—is intended to be visually obtrusive and heavy in contrast to the intricateness of the Chippendale furniture pieces. The black color which comes from the stained oak suggests the permanence and prominence of the Caribbean influence within British identity.

NBO: You're of Jamaican and English heritage and grew up in Nottingham. How has this shaped your work and practice?

MC: My dual heritage has allowed me to observe society perhaps more broadly and critically. Nottingham has a large Black and minority population. It was one of the major cities for settling Caribbean communities during the Windrush generation [1948–1971] and in the years since then. It also has a significant South Asian diaspora population. My interactions with these communities have surely influenced my opinions about design and inform the way that I determine value in objects, which in turn influences the way that I understand my own contribution to material culture.

NBO: You've described your work as part of a social movement. What does that mean?

MC: We underestimate the power of material culture in influencing our attitudes, behaviors and social beliefs. We are beginning to question how the objects that we encounter frame a time in history and our future. Commercial product design and art can change perceptions and challenge ideas that have been uncritically ingrained within our psyche.

NBO: You're becoming a prominent designer and you've received several awards. What does this mean for your future practice and aspirations?

MC: It seems like two paths are emerging—a conceptual practice and a more commercial route. The conceptual practice holds a sense of exclusivity where people might be able to experience my work but not necessarily own it and engage with it every day. Having a presence in commercial design would allow me to contribute more directly to material culture. It is an opportunity to leave a legacy that speaks to how people understand their lives and objects in them. The recognition has offered me the space, options and freedom to move in the holistic direction I want for my practice. I intend to find my own space and path.

HANG IN THERE
How to make the best of a bad job.

Having to implement a project you dislike is the worst. With merry ease, some creative director or executive outlines their vision and then leaves for a month of lunches while you are tasked with making it real. Now, alas, the all-gray interior must be designed, the loathsome video must be shot, the accursed app must be coded.

You aren't alone. Very few of us have genuine creative control over what we do. So, how to proceed? The traditional guidance is to muddle on. Character, and professionalism, after all, are defined by how well we perform in suboptimal situations. This type of advice traces its roots to Stoic philosophy. Stoics taught that character and virtue should be pursued with near-inhuman indifference to circumstance. Marcus Aurelius, a Stoic and Roman emperor, lived by this rule: "No matter what anyone does or says, my job is to be good."

If we balk at any task that doesn't suit our preference, we can't call ourselves professionals. Take Jimi Hendrix. In 1967, the guitar virtuoso was enjoying critical acclaim in the UK, but was essentially unknown in the American market. Someone, likely his manager, decided it would be a good idea for him to tour with the Monkees, the treacly boy band of their era. Hendrix agreed (despite having publicly called their music "dishwater" that same year) and soon found himself performing "Purple Haze" before outraged teenyboppers, who booed him off the stage for seven nights straight. In many ways, Hendrix was stoic—he carried on, and the music he played each night has stood the test of time. The temporary embarrassment, and the childish judgment of the crowd, did not. And yet a human being can only take so much. On the eighth night, it is said, Hendrix finished his set, smashed his guitar on stage, and gave the crowd a one-finger salute.

We owe it to ourselves to follow through, and to make the best of a bad job. But if we find ourselves on a conveyor belt of bad jobs, and nobody listens to our valuable input, it may be time to smash the guitar. Moderation in all things, then, even professionalism.

WORDS
ASHER ROSS
PHOTO
JULIAN SONG

MUCH ADO ABOUT NOTHING
The case against busywork.

WORDS
SALA ELISE PATTERSON
PHOTO
SCOTTIE CAMERON

At one of my first office jobs, an especially buxom co-worker used to nap in plain sight every day after lunch. Sitting at her desk, she would fold her arms across her chest, rest her chin between her breasts—and sleep. She got away with it for years. Who knows if management thought she was working, but she drew neither a second glance nor reprimand because it looked as though she was. Appearing busy got her off the hook from actually being busy.

It was a behavior management encouraged inadvertently by doling out busywork, those staple office activities meant to occupy people's time despite not generating an ounce of value for the employee or for the company's bottom line. Compile a pointless report, proofread a document no one else will ever read, call a meeting to plan a meeting.

Busywork thrives where a frenzied office is equated with a productive one. In these workplaces, every manager fears that one unproductive staff member will infect the entire office with indolence. It's the corporate equivalent of former New York City Mayor Rudolph Giuliani's broken window doctrine, which posited that even minimal signs of urban decay create an environment that encourages crime. But Giuliani got it wrong, as do managers: Human beings need restorative downtime.

The importance placed on keeping busy at work does have some merit: Productivity is linked to output, which is linked to profit. "Ever since a clock was first used to synchronise labour in the 18th century, time has been understood in relation to money," *The Economist* reported in 2014. But at some point, the theory was perverted, and the appearance of productivity became an acceptable substitute for the real thing.

What's surprising is how a practice that is so demoralizing to staff, not to mention pointless, continues to persist. But people are starting to game the game. Just Google "Ways to look busy at work": Disable the sleep mode on your computer, power walk nowhere in particular with a scowl on your face, sigh loudly and often, open Microsoft Excel. While it is encouraging that strategies have expanded beyond napping on your boobs, wouldn't it be nice to be granted time to do absolutely nothing in peace?

WORDS
ROBERT ITO
PHOTO
PIERROT

So you want to become a fossil, perhaps in the hopes that some anthropologist, years on, will come upon your mineralized remains. Setting the specific whys aside, do any of us have a say in who gets to be preserved in the geologic record?

Unfortunately for individuals interested in this particular strain of immortality, becoming a fossil isn't easy. As estimated by Bill Bryson in *A Short History of Nearly Everything*, of the trillions of creatures that have shuffled and slithered and swum across our planet since the dawn of time, less than one-tenth of 1% have had the good dumb luck to become fossils. The vast majority of animals and plants live, die and decompose leaving nary a trace.

But there are a few ways to increase one's chances. You can try to work things so that your body is buried under a lot of soil or ash (flash floods and volcanic eruptions can help there), so that wolves or condors can't eat your bones before the fossilization process even begins. Drowning in a body of water where your remains can be covered up with sediment, far out of reach of predators and the elements, also ups your odds (the "covering up with sediment" part is key here, given that there are hungry fish eager to get at you underwater, too). And assuming the point of all of this is to have your fossilized remains found by somebody thousands of years hence, you should try to die somewhere deep enough for you to fossilize, but not so deep that no one ever finds you.

Even if all of those other elements fall perfectly into place—the sediment and quick burial, the avoidance of predators and eventual discovery by some future digger—the fossilization process still takes a minimum of 10,000 years, by definition. That's a lot to think about, so don't rush. You've got a whole lifetime to plan your eventual demise.

HOW TO BECOME A FOSSIL
A short guide to self-preservation.

FEATURES:

Words
DOREE SHAFRIR
Photography
EMMA TRIM
Styling
JÈSS MONTERDE

Yoga with

Adriene

The internet's best friend is—finally— finding her own flow.

(above) Mishler wears a jumpsuit and tank top by MONSE.
(previous left) She wears a jacket by TOM FORD and a bodysuit by PARADE.
(previous right) She wears a bodysuit by RUI ZHOU.

During the first few months of the pandemic—those early, scary, pre-vaccine, schools-are-closed days, when we were all still figuring out how to navigate working from home and (possibly) taking care of kids and not going completely insane—there was one woman, it seemed, who had the capacity to lead us all through the wilderness. That woman was Adriene Mishler, better known as the yoga instructor behind the YouTube channel Yoga with Adriene.

Before the pandemic, Mishler had accumulated a devoted following of a few million, but as soon as lockdown hit, her follower count exploded and she was anointed as a kind of yogic Queen of Quarantine, with her faithful dog, Benji, as court jester.[1] She was hailed as the savior of a stressed-out populace, who flocked to her calm demeanor and straightforward videos with titles like "Yoga for Anxiety and Stress" and "Yoga for Self-Respect." Her juggernaut has shown no signs of stopping; since the beginning of the pandemic, she's doubled the follower count on her YouTube channel—where all the content is free—to 11 million, and has more than 50,000 subscribers to her paid app, Find What Feels Good, where she does a monthly vlog for members and she and other practitioners post video tutorials.

It seemed like a lot for one person to take on. And so, when Mishler joins a Zoom call with me one afternoon in May, I search her face for signs of the burnout she says she suffered last summer, when she decided she needed a break and packed Benji into her car and drove 2,000 miles from her home in Austin, Texas, to the Pacific Northwest for a month of downtime. (As soon as she got there, she got a call that her mother had had a stroke back in Austin, and she returned to Texas the next day.)

Almost immediately, Mishler tells me that she's just come from therapy. "I have a terrible habit of wearing my heart on my sleeve, which of course is a lovely thing, but there are some moments where it can be beautiful to keep things that are vulnerable quiet," she says. Mishler, who is 38, has expressive brown eyes and a deliberate voice, the kind that invites you in, even over a screen. "But today, I'll just share, with my heart on my sleeve, that I actually pushed our interview because I had scheduled a counseling session on Zoom. And then I thought, Oh no, how wise is it to move from an hour with my new therapist directly to an interview? The old me would have thought, That sounds terrible, because what place will I be in? But the current me was just like, You know what, as long as there's a little moment, just to have a breath in between the Zooms, then we can collect ourselves and reconnect to ourselves so that we can show up."

Hair & Makeup: Kelsey James. Styling Assistant: Inés Itsaso.

(1)   As well as making cameos in Mishler's YouTube tutorials, Benji stars in the animated series *Be Like Benji*, a guided meditation aid for children available on the Find What Feels Good app. In one episode, Benji learns to "box breathe" after getting stressed, while in another, Mishler teaches him how to calm down when he has "the zoomies" before bed. In 2020, he also starred in *Vote With Benji*, an animation encouraging subscribers to participate in the democratic process.

After years of being the person who taught others how to breathe and to take moments for themselves, Mishler seems—finally—ready to do that for herself. "This is a big moment for me," she says. "I'm finally giving myself permission to acknowledge that I haven't done a really good job of caring for myself first." She's soft-spoken and thoughtful as she says this. "When I feel a little off, I don't want to go 'perform Adriene.' I don't want to perform strong. That doesn't do my community or this opportunity that I've been given justice."

> " When I feel a little off, I don't want to go 'perform Adriene.' I don't want to perform strong."

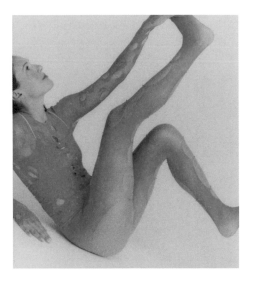

She had been honing the performance for a long time before she and a business partner, Chris Sharpe, decided to launch Yoga with Adriene on YouTube in 2012. After quitting high school and earning a GED diploma, Mishler became a yoga teacher at a theater in Austin where she was a repertory member. When the theater lost its lease in 2016, Mishler lost her teaching space. Now, a decade later, she co-owns her own yoga studio in Austin called Practice Yoga Austin and the YouTube channel is stronger than ever.

Many of her early videos focused on specific poses—pigeon, bridge, high lunge—along with the occasional vlog ("Yoga Pants and Other Yoga Questions Answered!"). She soon branched out into more thematic videos, like "Dorm Room Yoga" and "Yoga for the Winter Blues," but Mishler's most popular video of all time is the 20-minute "Yoga for Complete Beginners," which has more than 45 million views.[2] And while the production values may be a bit higher on her more recent videos, she really hasn't deviated much from the formula that initially brought her success. Watching her early videos, there's the familiar clear, confident voice, the way she refers to everyone watching as "my friends," the down-to-earth,

(left) Mishler wears a bodysuit by RUI ZHOU.
(below) She wears a top by ZELL, a bodysuit by PARADE and tights by WOLFORD.

(above)   She wears a balaclava by SANDY LIANG and a sweater and earrings by PATOU.
(right)   She wears a bodysuit by RUI ZHOU.

I-don't-take-myself-too-seriously vibe. This is not the yoga teacher who goes on a 10-minute digression at the beginning of class about a book she's reading; she's friendly, but ultimately Mishler is here to teach yoga.

I am one of her millions of students. Having dabbled here and there in Mishler's offerings pre-pandemic, once lockdown began, I was all in. Every night, after I put my toddler to bed, I'd turn off the lights in my office, turn on some LED candles and do a short restorative or evening yoga class. It was one of the only things during that time that took me out of what was happening around me. Ending my day with Adriene felt like a salve for my soul.

It's easy to see why Mishler might feel she had to "perform strong." The comments on her videos tend to range from effusive to rapturous. A not-untypical comment on a March video reads, in part: "I can proudly declare now that I am totally free from the depression prison.... Thank you so much, Adriene and all of the people in this community for being part of my journey to the world of light." To be told that you and your 26-minute "Upper Body" yoga video have saved someone's mental health is, of course, rewarding, but it also comes with incredible pressure.

When I ask Mishler what she attributes her success to, she gets a little uncomfortable. "I want to make a joke right now and say Benji," she says. But she thinks about it a little more and says, "We just do not get in a lot of spaces anymore to practice being ourselves and letting ourselves really see ourselves. And so all I can think of is that maybe people can feel me trying to do that. I know I probably annoy the shit out of a lot of people, but obviously a lot of people are showing up to practice. It's not me at all. It's not Benji at all. It's that [moment of] 'Ooh, we got one little spark that was like, I'm awesome.'"

(2) Speaking to *The Guardian* in 2018, Mishler was upfront about how she experimented with optimizing video titles for clicks. Sharpe, her business partner, had encouraged her to trial "Yoga for Weightloss" and they found it performed depressingly well.

Mishler's trajectory could have gone in a very different direction—she could have the branded videos and sponsored Instagram posts for protein powders that are standard in influencer culture. Instead, there's still a distinctly lo-fi element to both her videos and her social media. You do get the sense that a good friend is talking to you, not one of the most popular yoga teachers in the world. And it never feels like she's selling anything; yes, she wears clothing by her one of her partners, Adidas, in her videos, but her Instagram ads for the brand feel distinctly unpretentious.

Mishler says that while she "shied away from" being an influencer, she's now getting more focused on other business avenues. "I used to never talk about the business because I didn't want people to think about that or focus on that," she says. "But it seems dishonest to not name that." For many years, Mishler says, she and Sharpe "both felt like we didn't want to market anything to anyone. We are creative people and we wanted to create a place where we could own everything and be in control of everything."

The Find What Feels Good app had been active since 2015, but it was the pandemic that "gave me permission to go ahead and sell this thing." She saw new fitness apps launching practically every day and star instructors moving their classes online. "I just felt like, You know what? I think it's finally time to show people that we have this thing." The app is now grow-

> " I used to never talk about the business . . . I didn't want people to focus on that, but it seems dishonest to not name it."

ing, with classes in curvy yoga, kid yoga and meditation, and even green smoothie recipes. "My dream is that the Find What Feels Good platform really becomes like a *Sesame Street* for all kinds of teachers to come and share their work—a really diverse, fun, loving, creative mix of good leaders and good followers for the community to count on," she says.

Still, ultimately, she's trying to get back to herself, to figure out who Adriene-qua-Adriene is, and whether the path she's chosen is sustainable. She's been spending more time in Mexico City—her mother is Mexican—and has scaled back the number of videos she does.[3] "My partner asked me earlier this year what I like to do for fun. And I was like, *What?* It was a sweet conversation, but I think he was pointing out that I'm stuck in this, like, accomplishment-driven mode, even with the fun things." Mishler is contemplative for a moment, considering the possibility of a life not dominated by her practice. But even when she's thinking about this life beyond yoga, it somehow always circles back around to work. "Maybe bringing in more of that sense of play to nourish me will show up in the work," she concludes. "We'll see. We'll see!"

(3)   Mishler didn't speak Spanish while growing up, but learned her mother's first language as an adult. She founded a retreat in Mexico with Spanish teacher Sonia Gil that combines language learning and yoga, because she believes the two processes are inherently similar: both take you on journeys you might not anticipate.

An exclusive excerpt from our new book, *Kinfolk Islands.*

WORDS
LAURA RYSMAN
PHOTOS
CONSTANTIN MIRBACH

PONZA: Swimming and snacking on a volcanic coastline.

Rising sharply from the topaz surface of the Tyrrhenian Sea, the Italian island of Ponza has never lost its primeval aura. Though its port towns today have tight clusters of confetti-colored houses, Ponza's beaches are backed by embankments of raw lava petrified into striking shapes—a natural monument to the earth in its formative years, and a reminder of how this outpost looked to the Etruscans and Greeks who arrived here on early explorations of the area.

"We're out here in the middle of the sea, following in the footsteps of Ulysses and reconnecting with the philosophy of the ancient Greeks," says eminent Roman artist (and protégé of Cy Twombly's) Alberto Di Fabio, who purchased a remote property on Ponza a decade ago, transforming the white stucco home over long summers into a refuge from urban life. "This place is where I go to dream of more analog times," he says with a smile.

Though Di Fabio has apartments and studios in Rome and New York, his cave home on Ponza is where the painter found he was able to settle into a contemplative frame of mind. Visitors here are left enraptured by the purity of nature, he says. Di Fabio's neighbors are agriculturalists committed to growing in harmony with the land, and whose ventures include the acclaimed vineyard of Antiche Cantine Migliaccio, where ancestral methods and the Biancolella grapes (for centuries grown only on the Pontine Islands, of which Ponza is the largest) produce wines redolent of hawthorn flowers and the terrain's igneous flavor.

The wine is a natural match for Ponza's culinary delicacies, including linguine c'o Fellone, which is made with the island's native spider crabs, local red shrimp (often eaten raw), fresh-caught anchovies served with cherry tomatoes, and cicerchie, a flat pea that grows wild here.

Di Fabio spends his summer months on Ponza "reading, writing and gathering energy for new ideas," even occasionally painting, but when he takes a break from his ruminations, he heads to the dockside Bar Tripoli for an aperitivo and views of sailboats bobbing in rows on the water nearby. He may also duck into Hotel Chiaia di Luna where, gazing from the poolside terrace at the rift between two hills opening to a stretch of sea, "the sunset is incomparable." Around the central Piazza Carlo Pisacane, dinner is best taken at Ristorante L'Aragos-

(above)
From Porto di Ponza, you can take a boat out to the tiny island of Palmarola, and swim or snorkel into vaulted grottoes set back into high cliffs.

ta, at Ristorante Eéa (Ponza is thought to be cited as Eéa in Homer's *Odyssey*) or at Gennarino a Mare, where the dining terrace is built right into the waters along the shore. For dinner with "vistas of faraway horizons," where the sea and sky can be appreciated in vast expanses, Di Fabio suggests the westward-facing Tramonto (sunset) restaurant, situated high above the hills in the exact center of the island.

The artist also recommends visiting other regions on the island, engaging with the traditional atmosphere of its smaller towns. "If you want to experience Italy as it was in the 1950s and '60s, you have to go to Le Forna," he says of the area at the island's northern tip. Here he suggests Ristorante Punta Incenso, or Da Igino—"the absolute top, with fish served roasted or salt-baked that comes directly from the fishermen working in the Cala Fonte bay there." Di Fabio always stops to appreciate the view of the fishermen's old wooden boats sheltered by the dramatic rocks curving around the cove. Nearby, he likes to swim at the Cala Gaetano, a crystalline inlet with a rocky shore surrounded by prickly pears and blackberry brambles. It can be reached only by the ambitious—the steep climb counts over three hundred stairs—but it keeps the beach uncrowded. At one of the few sandy beaches on the island, Cala Feola, the Ristorante La Marina is unmissable, as are the natural pools that have formed along the shoreline. Di Fabio also makes the journey to Bar Zanzibar to enjoy a drink by the pebble beach of Santa Maria, encircled by the town's colorful houses.

At Frontone, a sandy cove surrounded by small verdant cliffs, Di Fabio likes to dine and stargaze at Da Enzo, where tables are set out on the rocks by the water—the owner transports guests to their table in a rowboat. In the daytime, the nearby Ristoro da Gerardo serves its homey dishes in a more rural setting, "a paradise on the hillside with chickens and goats wandering around you," as the artist describes it. The owner has even set up a self-made ethnographic museum in one room, laying out the antique tools and folk art of life in old Ponza, with the scythes and fishing nets they've used to collect their food and models of the boats they've used to sail around these remote waters—all glimpses of an analog time that feels much closer on Ponza's ancient shores.

KINFOLK

ISLANDS

(above)   This story is an exclusive excerpt from our forthcoming book, *Kinfolk Islands*. Pre-order at Kinfolk.com now, or shop in stores worldwide from October 25.

What are the
media ethics of
sending ordinary
people viral?

ESSAY:
BUZZ KILL

Words
RACHEL CONNOLLY

Sometimes a certain personal story will strike a deeply relatable chord with the collective, perhaps because it speaks to a fundamental element of the human condition—like feeling out of place, lonely or misunderstood—or because it seems to exemplify a familiar group dynamic. Maybe it relates to a wider social or political issue in which many feel invested. Or it may be a situation in which someone has been treated unfairly; the premise of fairness is often very stirring.

Narrative nonfiction—a style of journalism in which true stories involving real people are told in the entertaining fashion of a novel, rather than via straight reporting—has boomed over the past few decades. *This American Life*, which pioneered using this form in a radio context, has over two million weekly listeners. Salacious articles about striking protagonists written for magazines like *Vanity*

up in Woodstock, Alabama, on the premise of investigating an alleged murder, after being repeatedly emailed by a resident of the town, John B. McLemore. Reed deduced that the murder had not taken place and recorded hours of conversations with McLemore in the process. When McLemore died by suicide while the podcast was in production, the series changed direction. Reed used earlier conversations recorded with McLemore (some off the record) and other residents of the town, to tell the story of his suicide and lifestyle.

S-Town was hugely popular; the themes of isolation, feeling like an outsider, and depression resonated widely. It has been downloaded more than 90 million times since it was released in 2017. This brought a huge degree of public interest in McLemore's life and the town of Woodstock. Cheryl Dodson, a friend of McLemore's who works in

" I didn't know what a podcast was. When it went viral and they were playing it at work on a loudspeaker, it was completely surreal."

Fair, *The New Yorker* or *New York Magazine* are regularly optioned for film or documentary purposes.[1]

The form has long been popular; Truman Capote's 1966 nonfiction novel *In Cold Blood*, which told the story of the gruesome murder of a Kansas family, was a bestseller and is still a required text on many school syllabi.[2] But narrative nonfiction is ethically controversial, particularly when you add social media to the equation. The potential for virality has created a strange ecosystem in which thousands or millions of strangers can discuss the individuals at the center of a story in real time. The analogous quality of these stories can make those involved seem less like people and more like characters; the online mob can choose a villain and lobby for their punishment.

One recent example of a story that turned normal people into microcelebrities was the *S-Town* podcast. This series saw producer Brian Reed turn

the local library and is featured in *S-Town*, says, "I didn't know what a podcast was when I was originally interviewed. I had no idea. When it went viral and they were playing it at work on a loudspeaker, it was completely surreal."

Dodson says that when *S-Town* originally aired, she received harassment online from fans who believed, through the bond they felt with McLemore via the podcast, that there may have been signs he was suicidal that his friends had missed. As she points out, when people associate strongly with an impactful story they can forget that they don't truly know those involved. "The seven hours

(1)   The viral story of Anna Sorokin, who fooled the New York elite into thinking she was a German heiress, has spawned a memoir, a BBC podcast and a Netflix series. Unlike so many of the subjects of virality, however, Sorokin has profited from the attention: Netflix reportedly paid the imprisoned con artist $320,000 for the rights to adapt her story.

(2)   *In Cold Blood* is seen as a pioneering text in the true crime genre. Capote made the unusual decision to hear the killers' version of events and became emotionally embroiled in their fate.

[of the podcast] gave people a relationship with John but it was not in comparison to our 20-year friendship," she explains.

The privacy invasion was particularly hard while grieving the loss of her friend. "People would argue with me and I would question myself about my friendship," she says. But Dodson has used the momentum around *S-Town* to help raise awareness of suicide risks. She is now the president of the Alabama Suicide Prevention and Resources Coalition and runs Zoom classes for suicide prevention training known as Question, Persuade, Refer. She says the story of her relationship with John is familiar to many due to the podcast and that it has helped her connect with people from all over the world in the online training sessions.

" The cost is often people feeling betrayed or unduly exposed. That isn't always a fair price for our entertainment."

Dodson's drive to make something positive out of this strange form of celebrity is admirable. But some of these stories, which turn normal people into totems, don't seem to have a silver lining. Last year, the *New York Times Magazine* ran "Who Is the Bad Art Friend?," a story detailing the legal wrangling of a pair of women who knew each other from a writing workshop and were embroiled in a plagiarism dispute.[3] A dossier of private text messages depicted one of the women, Sonya Larson, and her friends talking about the other, Dawn Dorland. Dorland unearthed the texts during the legal proceedings and they were included in the article.

(3)   The conflict at the heart of "Who Is the Bad Art Friend?" is convoluted, but centers on Larson's decision to write a short story criticizing a woman who donates a kidney—something that Dorlan had recently done—as suffering from a savior complex. Writing in *The Guardian*, Emma Brockes summed up this genre of story: "Here are some people you've never heard of—and, guess what, they're awful!"

(4)   In his piece, Kolker appears bemused by the popularity of "Who Is the Bad Art Friend?" "I remember thinking that the case was so complex and the issues so insular that it would be hard to get anyone interested," he writes.

This led to many of those involved being removed from their roles at GrubStreet, the nonprofit writing organization where they all met. Discussions about which of the women was in the wrong rumbled on social media for weeks, with many articles, blog posts, Twitter threads and podcasts devoted to arguing one way or the other. Opinion was split, and neither party emerged unscathed.

The audience response to such a piece is unpredictable. Robert Kolker, the journalist who wrote "Who Is the Bad Art Friend?" addressed this after it went viral. "Neither I nor any of the editors involved in the piece expected it to turn into Twitter's favorite parlor game," he wrote. "I feel a lot of the debate that continues to swirl across Twitter risks flattening the piece into a tale of good guys and bad guys."[4]

Even in circumstances where someone becomes a temporary public figure ostensibly for their own benefit, the loss of privacy can be devastating. Francisco Garcia, a journalist who wrote *If You Were There: Missing People and the Marks They Leave Behind*, a book investigating the missing people's crisis, has interviewed people who have found themselves in the middle of a social media campaign when presumed missing. These people aren't allegories exactly, but there is a parallel in the attention they receive.

"The people I spoke with who'd experienced this kind of online scrutiny invariably referred to a loss of agency," writes Garcia over email. "There are no real guidelines or rules of engagement with these things, and certainly no 'aftercare' for the person at the heart of it."[5]

Garcia says it is hard to think of easy solutions to the problems wrought by viral attention, in terms of reporting guidelines: "I think a clear problem, though, is when these pieces are written in a deliberate viral register, clearly meant to scandalize. It makes for entertaining narrative nonfiction, but the cost is often people feeling betrayed or unduly exposed. And that isn't always a fair price for our entertainment, depending on the subject and the story."

Janet Malcolm famously addressed the ethical conflict at the heart of nonfiction in her 1990 book *The Journalist and the Murderer*. She says that the practice is "morally indefensible. . . . Like the credulous widow who wakes up one day to find the charming young man and all her savings gone,

so the consenting subject of a piece of nonfiction writing learns—when the article or book appears—his hard lesson."

Malcolm argues that, since a journalist chooses how to frame the events they describe, there is a power imbalance between the journalist and their subject which is inherently exploitative. In the three decades since the book came out, social media has allowed the audience to publish their own sense of a narrative too, without any expectation of professional obligations or consequences. "It's funny," Dodson says, when we speak about her experience of online harassment by *S-Town* fans, "I actually met one of them in person, and I did not know them but they recognized me and they were apologizing for what they did to me a few years ago. I have learned that when they are face to face with you, it's not the same as what they do to you online."

(5) In his 2015 book *So You've Been Publicly Shamed*, Jon Ronson writes about the growing number of companies that offer reputation management services for people who have found themselves unwittingly in the public eye. Ronson follows one woman's journey as the company Reputation.com attempts to wipe an embarrassing viral photo from the internet by flooding Google with other content about her.

From the Outer Hebrides to central London, *Catherine Lock* is celebrating the crafts heritage of Great Britain.

WORDS
MALAIKA BYNG
PHOTOGRAPHY
CECILIE JEGSEN

AT WORK WITH: The New Craftsmen

A walk around The New Craftsmen's London showroom is a journey across the British Isles. Each object is a portal to a place and its making traditions. In one corner of the lofty Arts and Crafts-era building, a spindle-back bench by Bibbings & Hensby transports you to Wales via the region's Windsor chair making tradition. Suspended over a table nearby is a lamp made from a bird's nest–like mass of heather by Annemarie O'Sullivan. It whisks you up to the wilds of Scotland's Orkney Islands, where people have long made household objects from the native shrub.

Amid these storied pieces, Catherine Lock is sitting at an oak table, drinking tea from a ceramic mug. "In your working day, when you're glued to technology, holding a handmade cup by a maker you know and from a place you've heard of, just makes life feel better," says the creative director, who is a slow but passionate speaker. "It makes the tea taste better too." Behind her, plates by Oxford-based ceramicist Dylan Bowen line the wall, each emblazoned with gestural streaks of clay slip. "To me, craft is all about an expression of humanity."

With her team of 18, Lock curates and commissions objects for the home by highly skilled craftspeople. "Many makers just follow a tradition, but we look for artists who can add playfulness and curiosity," she explains. The showroom—a 19th-century former workshop for makers of leather breeches on Mayfair's North Row—is a tranquil haven where natural materials abound, no two pieces of furniture or ceramic are the same and imperfections are welcomed. All this feels like a direct riposte to the throwaway culture of Oxford Street, the fast-fashion mecca to which North Row runs parallel. Here, time slows down. "We see people visibly relax,

drop their shoulders and take a breath when they enter because it's such a visceral, sensual space," Lock says. "We've even had a visitor arrive on horseback. He didn't buy anything, but we ended up working with his saddlemaker."

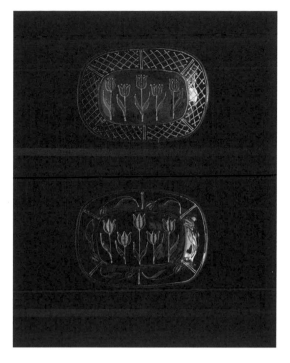

(above)
Slip Trailed Tulip Dishes by FITCH & MCANDREW.

It's typical of how relationships are formed in the close-knit craft world, where one conversation can lead to a whole network of collaborators. "I'm quite London-centric day-to-day, but if I'm traveling somewhere in the UK on my time off, I will always visit a maker we represent and keep an eye open for others in that area," says Lock. She has just returned from a whistle-stop tour of Scotland, where she dropped

in on ceramic artists James Rigler and Viv Lee in Glasgow, and the Begg x Co. textile mill near the town of Ayr. "Visiting a maker's studio is the best way to understand their skills, motivations and ambitions. Often, I'll spot something on a shelf—an old idea that they have forgotten about—and I'll see the potential for our customers. You've got to be nosy."

Lock studied fashion design at university, but the industry wasn't a comfortable fit for a student drawn to timeless workwear—fishermen's sweaters and farmers' smocks—rather than trend cycles. After university, she spent 15 years as a homeware developer for mass-market retailers including Habitat and supermarket giant Sainsbury's. But she became fed up with the uniformity and disposability she was seeing. Certain changes she saw in the food world while at Sainsbury's suggested that a different path was possible for homeware. "Twelve years ago, we were seeing a shift in how people bought food—they were going to farmers markets, meeting producers and buying local produce," Lock explains. "It was becoming clear that, even in a supermarket, they were willing to pay more for sausages if they knew the farm they came from and the breed of a pig. My feeling was that this attitude was going to go beyond food. We were at a tipping point."

An idea from her college days about beautifully made pieces rooted in regional traditions kept playing on her mind. "I knew this stuff existed, but I wasn't sure where," she says. So, in 2010, she rented out her London apartment, packed her bag and set off on a craft pilgrimage across the UK.

Lock met lace-makers on the Shetland Islands; fishermen "gansey" knitters in the Outer Hebrides; scissor-makers in Sheffield; and wrestlers in Cumberland and

(previous)   Hakeme Casserole Dish III and Ying Ching Serving Bowl by MATTHEW FOSTER, Wood Ash Faceted Flask IV by ADAM ROSS.
(left)   Stitched Sideboard by AIMEE BETTS & GARETH NEAL, *A Turning Collage* by JO WATERHOUSE, Pilotis Side Table by MALGORZATA BANY, Bowl by ALEXANDER DE VOL and Log Basket by OTIS INGRAMS.

Westmorland who wore hand-embroidered shirts. What she found was a series of distinct craft practices, rooted in their regions and inflected by local histories and materials, but without a clear commercial platform. "I came back absolutely buzzing," she says. "It was a very self-indulgent, personal journey."

Still, it didn't take her long to turn her discoveries into a business. Back in London, she teamed up with Mark Henderson and Natalie Melton, who shared a background in supporting makers and a belief that people wanted objects with narrative and personality in their lives. They became her co-founders; Yelena Ford, the company's managing director, joined in 2014.

Many of the crafts Lock found on her journey had humble origins, born out of everyday needs, but the team realized that for these labor-intensive practices to be sustainable in today's world, the objects had to have a certain price tag. The New Craftsmen's collections are humble in origin but not in price, as the showroom's well-heeled Mayfair location makes clear. "I was scared of the word 'luxury' because it was a different world back then—luxury meant polished, smooth and shiny, without much personality," says Lock. "My own sensibility was more wobbly and human. I was interested in the aesthetic underdogs, like slipware pottery, which is earthy, hearty and functional, with a rich history." When they opened the first pop-up shop for The New Craftsmen in Mayfair two years later, they offered an altogether more textured alternative to Mayfair's prevailing gloss.

One of the first people they tapped was Gareth Neal, a furniture designer with a deep interest in rural vernaculars. They still work with him today. The New Craftsmen dispatched him to Scotland to meet Kevin Gauld, who makes straw-backed Orkney chairs—a tradition on the Heritage Crafts Association's Red List of Endangered Crafts in the UK. "I could see there was a marketplace for them, if the shape could be made a little more contemporary and Kevin could repeat it at a slightly faster pace," Lock says. "That's where Gareth came in." The resulting Brodgar Occasional Chair is now in the permanent collection of the Victoria & Albert Museum.

After several pop-up ventures, The New Craftsmen moved into its permanent home on North Row in 2014. Lock and the team switch up the furniture and objects about four times a year, hosting regular exhibitions.

Since her travels around the UK, the public's appetite for the handmade has changed radically. In England alone, the total market for craft was 26.5 million people in 2010, but by 2020 it had boomed to 38.1 million, according to the UK Crafts Council.[1] Instagram was still in its infancy when The New Craftsmen launched. "We didn't even have an account initially but today, Instagram has changed the crafts scene beyond recognition," Lock says. "Anyone can make and sell their work directly to their followers."

Competition from Instagram and the new breed of amateur makers could have eroded sales: If anyone can be a ceramicist, why would people pay upwards of £250 for a teapot? "Communicating the skills of our artists and the 10,000 hours of practice required to be a master is an inherent part of what we do because we have to justify our prices," she says. To sidestep social media competition, Lock works with artists to develop exclusive pieces.

Did she join the masses and start making during the pandemic? "I've tried before, but within an hour of attempting to throw a pot, I realized I didn't have the patience, so I played the piano during lockdown instead," Lock says. "Being a craftsperson requires dedication."

Over the last decade, interior designers have become increasingly hungry for craft, with hotel collaborations gaining momentum. When guests wake up at Heckfield Place in Hampshire, for example, they will find textured water glasses by Jochen Holz on their nightstands, and lighting by glassmaker Michael Ruh in their bathrooms, thanks to a 2018 partnership with BTW design studio. Meanwhile, visitors to the Whitby Hotel in New York can marvel at the skills of 20 British basket makers overhead while they enjoy a cocktail at the bar. Lock's dream project would be to transform a home from top to bottom, so that every surface is handmade, much like our interiors would have been hundreds of years ago. She'll need to find a homeowner with deep pockets.

Lock's hunch that things were shifting back in 2010 proved right: Craft is now the zeitgeist, with legions of high-profile devotees, including pottery fanatic Seth Rogen and embroiderer Greta Thunberg. But the creative director bristles at the word "trend" just like she did at the term "fashion" all those years ago as a student. "We want our collections to endure the test of time," she says. Thunberg would approve.

> " I was interested in the aesthetic underdogs."

(1) According to the UK Crafts Council, almost a third (32%) of today's British craft buyers are aged under 35, making millennials the largest demographic in the market. In 2019, craft sales in the UK totaled over £3 billion (over $3.75 billion).

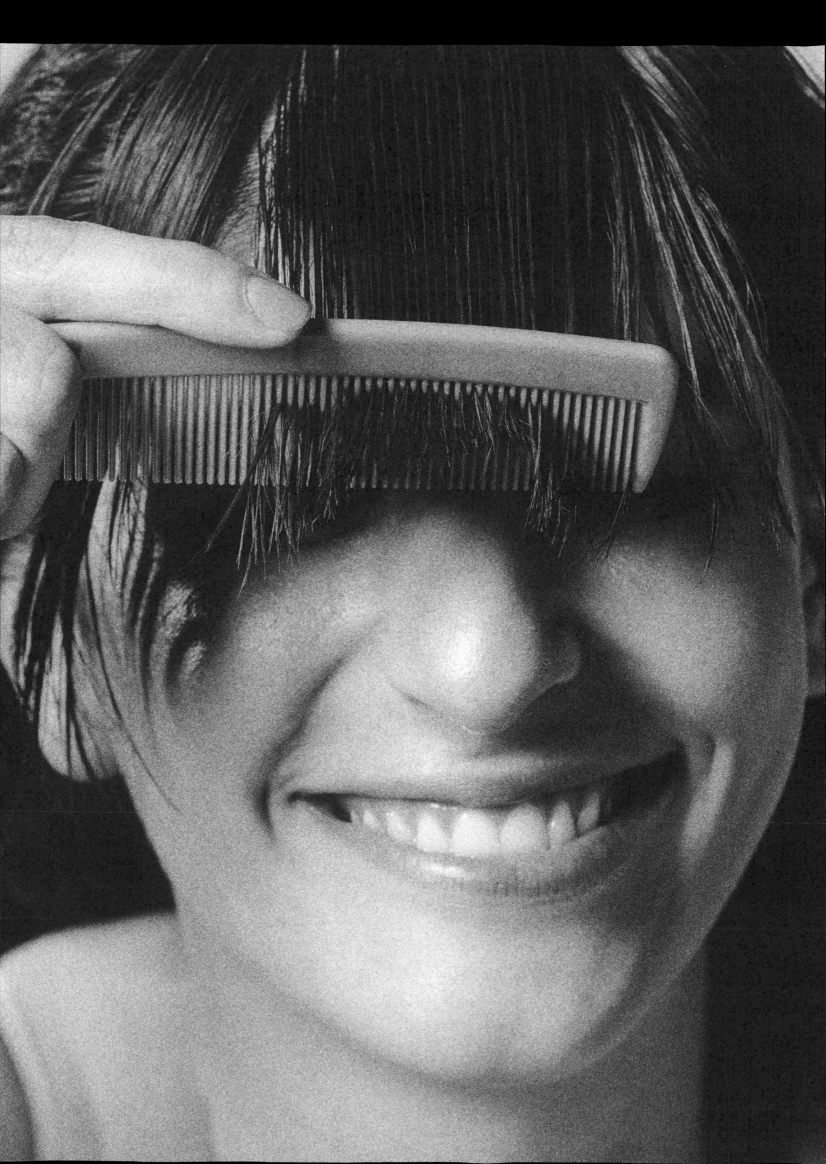

When getting ready
is half the fun.

79   WET LOOK

Photography
LAUREN BAMFORD
Styling
POPPY BUNTZ

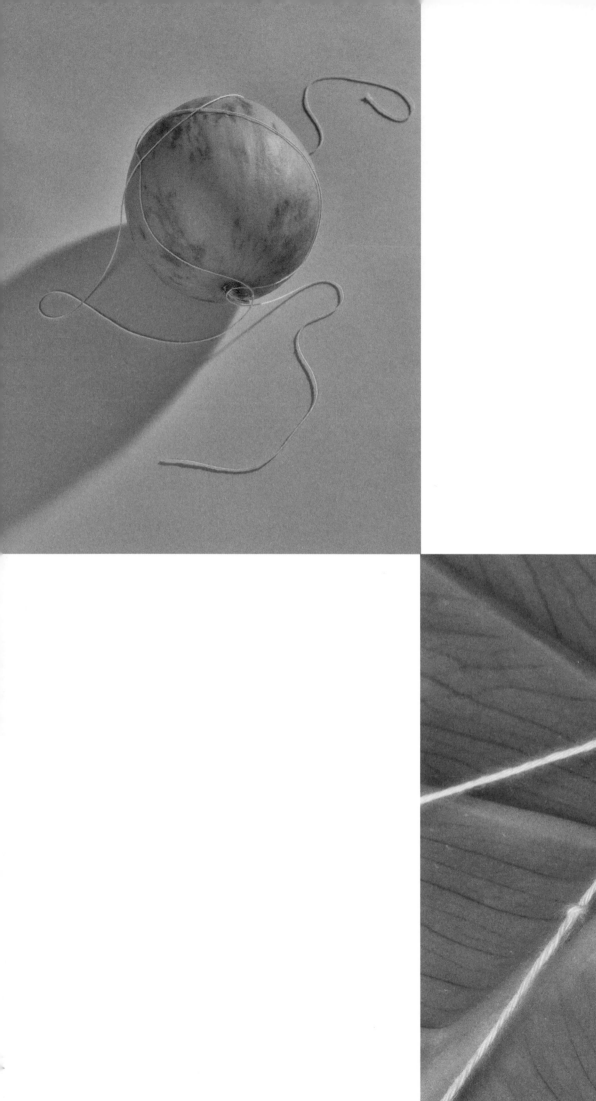

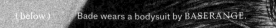

(above)   Bade wears a Ladymatic Co-Axial Chronometer 34mm watch by OMEGA.

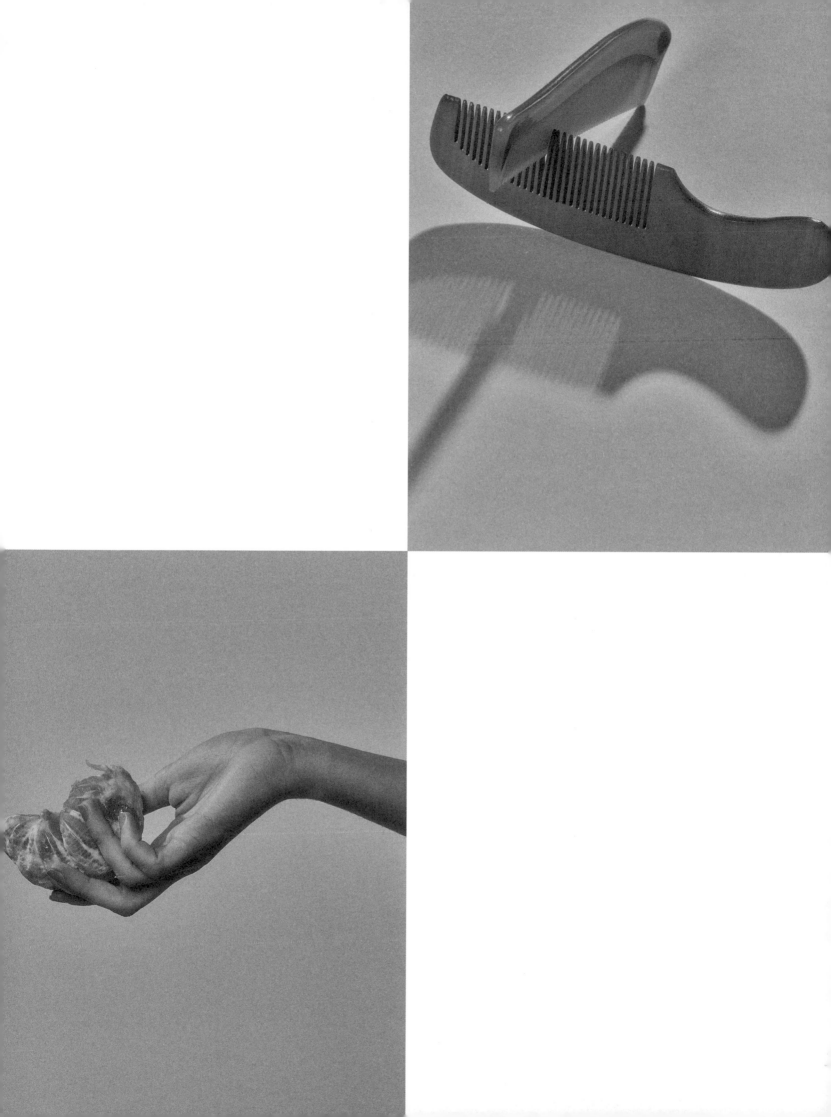

FEATURES

HOME TOUR: Ollivier & Gladys Chenel

A pas de deux
inside an antiques-filled
Paris apartment.

WORDS
GEORGE UPTON
PHOTOGRAPHY
ALIXE LAY

In Ollivier and Gladys Chenel's Paris apartment there is a 17th-century marble console, on which a series of objects have been carefully arranged: a second-century marble head, the fragment of a column from an ancient Roman monument, a ceramic dove by Pablo Picasso and a photograph of the Mediterranean coast taken from inside Adalberto Libera's iconic Villa Malaparte by François Halard. It's a neat cross-section of the eclectic mix of art, objects and antiquities that fill the couple's home in the historic city center.

For Ollivier and Gladys, though, the key to understanding their creative and collaborative approach to collecting is, in fact, a small work by the British artist John Stezaker. It hangs in the entryway and consists of two black-and-white photographs combined to create a single image of a man and a woman. "At first you see this as a collage of artifacts of the past," says Gladys. "You then realize that it forms quite a unique and surreal portrait of two people." In much the same way, their collection has grown to be a kind of double self-portrait, the product of their shared interests and the many years they have been together.

While their apartment might be filled with a wealth of art and objects, the Chenels don't see themselves as collectors. Serious collecting is left to their clients. The couple founded Galerie Chenel in 1999 along with Ollivier's brother, Adrien, specializing in ancient sculpture. "If we really started collecting antiques we would never sell anything, and that wouldn't be good for business," says Ollivier.

Most of the antiquities in the couple's apartment are on temporary loan from the gallery. But the ephemerality of their collection emphasizes the intimate and tactile relationship the couple has with these objects.

These are not investments that need to be carefully stored and never seen but works of art that are there to be studied and shared before they move on to a new home.

"They are sculptural objects. You want to see them from every side, so you have to touch them," says Gladys, spinning an Egyptian alabaster vase on the table in front of her. "It's always been important to us that this is a family apartment where people will feel comfortable and our kids can play, rather than a museum. Though it is something of a miracle that nothing has ever been broken."

The Chenels had been looking for the perfect place for a long time. They were renting typically Parisian, Haussmannian-style apartments but now they were looking to buy and wanted somewhere interesting and unusual to make it worthwhile. After searching for several years, they walked into this apartment inside a 17th-century building. "It had been empty for two years when we first saw it," Gladys says. "But you could tell it had a soul. As soon as I saw the original parquet floor, I knew we had to find a way to live here."

Just as in this historic part of Paris, which survived the extensive redevelopment of the city in the mid-19th century, little has changed in the apartment over the centuries. The previous owner had knocked through to the adjacent apartment in the 1970s but the original features—the painted ceilings, the vast marble fireplace, the parquet floor—had otherwise been left untouched.

"We wanted to find somewhere that we could adapt to, rather than adapting the house to fit us," Ollivier says. Their architectural interventions in the apartment were largely limited to converting the second entryway into a bedroom for their son and remodeling the bathrooms, which Gladys designed. Even the fabric covering the wall in the bedroom was left unchanged, informing the couple's approach to the decoration of the rest of the room.

> " This is a family apartment. It is a miracle that nothing has ever been broken."

FEATURES

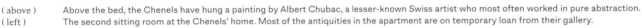

(above)   Above the bed, the Chenels have hung a painting by Albert Chubac, a lesser-known Swiss artist who most often worked in pure abstraction.
(left)   The second sitting room at the Chenels' home. Most of the antiquities in the apartment are on temporary loan from their gallery.

This is not to say that the apartment is a Louis XIV-era house museum. The couple may have restored the painted ceilings but the space has also been filled with modern and contemporary artwork and carefully chosen design pieces, such as the Pierre Augustin Rose sofa that curves across the living room and the Mario Bellini-designed Cassina table in the dining room. That it all works together with the ancient objects—which include a Corinthian capital, the top part of a column, upended to serve as a plinth—is a testament to the couple's careful approach. "We will never buy anything just because we've seen it in a catalog and like the look of it," Gladys says. "Behind every piece, there is a story."

The couple gives several examples: The Picasso ceramics are similar to those sold by Ollivier's father, who was also a dealer; the photorealistic drawing by Emmanuel Régent of a temple is from Nice, where the couple met; the antique narwhal tusk is a prized family object because their children used to think it came from a unicorn.

As at the gallery—where they have frequently held exhibitions of contemporary art, design and photography alongside ancient sculpture—the couple's dynamic approach to antiquities at home is a breath of fresh air, blowing the dust from a specialism that has been seen as traditional and elitist.

"We want to show how you can live with antiquities. They don't only have to be in a museum," Ollivier says.[1] "And it's such a joy to live with them," Gladys continues. "The pieces always look different in the morning light than in the afternoon. I think we would struggle to live without sculptures in our lives now. We will even take a piece or two with us on holiday."

The collecting of antiquities was at its height of popularity in the 19th century, when Greek, Roman and Egyptian artifacts were seen to associate their owner with the elevated ideals of ancient civilizations. Ollivier and Gladys' approach, however, is far more humble, rooted in a sense of wonder and passion for ancient sculpture that inspired them to open their gallery 23 years ago.

"Above all, we love architectural fragments," Ollivier says. "You can imagine the scale and spirit of a colossal building from a much smaller piece."

At Ollivier and Gladys' home, one also gets the sense of the scale of time from these antiquities, of the different owners and homes that they have passed through since they were created. Many have existed for more than 2,000 years and could go on existing for as long yet. "We are only guardians of these sculptures," Ollivier says. "In one or two generations, we'll be gone, though people will be able to find out that these objects once passed through us." "The best moments when we are researching the provenance of an object at the gallery are when we find it in a photograph from an old issue of *Connaissance des Arts* or *AD*," adds Gladys. "It's nice to think that maybe in 50 years, people will be looking through a magazine and see that their piece was once in this house."

(1) Galerie Chenel has sold ancient sculptures to some of the world's most important institutions, including the Metropolitan Museum of Art, the Boston Museum of Fine Arts, the British Museum and the Louvre Museum. The gallery is actually located opposite the Louvre, on Quai Voltaire.

Zawe

Words
HETTIE O'BRIEN
Photography
PELLE CRÉPIN

Ashton

Styling
HOLLY WHITE

Through writing, actor Zawe Ashton is slowly shifting her role from object to subject.

The work of a convincing performer is to make a practice of disjunction, blurring fact and fiction until it's no longer clear where the performance ends. Zawe Ashton, an actor and writer from East London, has been performing for so long that she sometimes feels as though she has "just woken up." "There has been this eye, this gaze, that has followed me since birth," she says. This is what it is to have grown up as a child actor, an experience that would be strange, were Ashton to have ever known anything different.

It's only now, at the age of 37, that Ashton feels she has managed to "reshuffle the cards," as she puts it. We're speaking over Zoom: Ashton from the northwest London home she shares with her fiancé, the actor Tom Hiddleston, and me from an office room that I describe, when she asks, as a "Zoom booth." "Are they the new thing? They sound sexy," Ashton says with characteristic provocation. "They sound like the new location for a fresh scandal to me. *It happened in a Zoom booth!*"

There is a sense that runs through Ashton's work of someone chafing at the limits of their discipline. She is best known in the US for her role in *Velvet Buzzsaw*, a satirical horror film set in the Los Angeles art world in which she starred alongside Jake Gyllenhaal. She grew up in Hackney, East London (her parents were both schoolteachers; her mother is Ugandan, her father English) and attended Anna Scher, a theater school in Islington that banned the words "star" and "fame" from the classroom: Stars burn out, Scher taught them, but the career of an actor persists regardless of fame.

Ashton's first notable role was in the British kids' TV show *The Demon Headmaster*. In her early 20s, she took bit parts in crime dramas and hospital soaps; her break came when she was cast, at 27, as the chaotic, drug-taking, straight-talking student Vod in the series *Fresh Meat*. One article from the time suggested Ashton was "the coolest thing on TV right now." But Ashton felt herself growing increasingly frustrated. "I hit a wall in my life—whether it was burnout, or [an] existential crisis, where I was like, Hold on a minute . . . . I've spent the past 30-something years performing, and I have no idea who for."

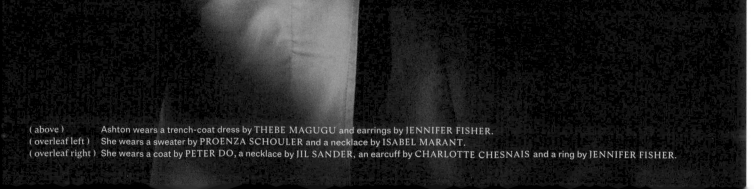

(above)   Ashton wears a trench-coat dress by THEBE MAGUGU and earrings by JENNIFER FISHER.
(overleaf left)   She wears a sweater by PROENZA SCHOULER and a necklace by ISABEL MARANT.
(overleaf right) She wears a coat by PETER DO, a necklace by JIL SANDER, an earcuff by CHARLOTTE CHESNAIS and a ring by JENNIFER FISHER.

What Ashton really wanted to do, she tells me, was to be a writer. In the basement, her mother still keeps a box of the stories Ashton wrote as a child, including one, from when she was six, about a dinosaur having breakfast with Elizabeth Taylor. "I think language, and how surreal and expressive language is, has always been part of my wanting to be in this world." So, alongside her acting jobs, Ashton wrote a play. *For All the Women Who Thought They Were Mad* centered on the experiences of Black women in the corporate workplace and was praised for its darkly comic study of prejudice when it was staged at the Hackney Showroom in 2019.[1] She also wrote a pilot for a TV drama about a woman having an early midlife crisis. "I was treated extremely badly at the hands of television executives," she says. The pilot was passed over, and Ashton "put it in a drawer because it was just too traumatic."

> " Hold on a minute. I've spent the past 30-something years performing, and I have no idea who for."

A book agent read that defunct script, and asked if Ashton would consider authoring something longer. "It's one of the hardest, best things I've done," she says of the resulting book, *Character Breakdown*, a playful, tragicomic account of an unnamed protagonist's acting career. "So much of my life has been scripted; so much commitment has been to saying other people's words and inhabiting other women," she explains. "I thought . . . I can sit down and write this without anyone giving me permission." Writing was an opportunity to stop acting—for a while. Ashton spent some time living in Margate, a blustery seaside town popular with people priced out of London. She nicknamed the book, which took two years to finish, "the cockroach in the nuclear disaster of my life." For a while, it felt like the only continuity she could grasp at.

Character Breakdown defies the very definition of the word *order*—it is composed of fragmentary conversations retold in a weaving chronology. The protagonist receives different character synopses that are irritatingly sexist (a silent woman in a civil rights protest, a sexy spy, a dead body on a mortuary slab). She takes calls from her agent, sips lukewarm wine, changes her hair to appease casting directors and remembers being bullied at school after first appearing on TV. It is loosely fictionalized: Ashton says that if the book seems like an "actor's memoir," she has "done something very wrong." "It was an attempt, or an opportunity, to try and crack open the difference between fact and fiction before slamming them wholeheartedly back together again," she explains.

(1) Ashton's play was formally innovative, using dreamlike sequences and time hops to bring a mystical resonance to the script's corporate setting. In the play, the stage is surrounded by a chorus of Black women who step in to comment on protagonist Joy's life and seek to protect her as it unravels. The play premiered at the same time as Ashton was acting in Harold Pinter's *Betrayal* on Broadway, opposite her now-fiancé, Tom Hiddleston.

Although magnified in the acting industry, the banal occur-rences of casual misogyny and racism that Ashton's protagonist endures resonate far beyond the book. "Thinking about acting be-came like a blueprint for a way that I could look at my experience as a woman in the world," she says. She missed her publisher's first deadline, a misstep that turned into a gift. By the time Ashton sub-mitted the manuscript, revelations of sexual violence in the film industry had started to break. "Me Too really reframed my writing completely, because I thought, No one is going to want to hear from an actress about stuff that's gone down and how it might relate to the wider world. And suddenly it was all anyone wanted to hear."

We're speaking a month before the release of *Mr. Malcolm's List*, a sugar-frosted Regency rom-com in which Ashton plays a lead role. The film revolves around the wayward schemes of Ashton's char-acter, Miss Julia Thistlewaite, and will please anyone who enjoyed *Bridgerton*.[2] In period-drama obsessed Britain, it would have been unthinkable for a mixed-heritage British woman to land this role even five years ago. The multiracial elite portrayed in *Mr. Malcolm's List* is a fantasy that omits the reality of colonial racism in Regency Britain, casting actors of color as dukes and duchesses. "There is a lucrative market .... for the depiction of racial difference in the absence of racial inequality," the British author and journalist Gary

Younge recently wrote of *Bridgerton*, taking issue with the genre. Ashton is critical of this argument. "What's crazy is there's only a handful of [similar] shows," she says. "When you get real diversity is when there are so many . . . . that some can show one aspect [of history], some can show another aspect, and this is a spectrum."

The protagonist of *Character Breakdown* reflects that "nothing good comes of being visible." Together with this film, and her forthcoming role as a Marvel villain, Ashton seems poised to become the kind of highly visible celebrity who occupies a different plane of existence: rich, distant and chauffeured.[3] Yet that's not how she comes across in person. She is open and disarming, throwing back bigger questions to those I ask. I wonder if she enjoys the control of writing in her own words, as opposed to speaking those of others. "It doesn't even feel like control," she says. Ashton tells me about the American visual artist Lorraine O'Grady (about whom she made a film for the Tate). "She wanted to play with the idea of being subject and object," Ashton says. "You want to shift the lens, shift the perspective on your work and life as much as you can. And that's how I feel."

(2)   Director Emma Holly Jones has said that her casting choices were inspired by *Hamilton* rather than *Bridgerton*, although the storyline has far more in common with the latter. The action hinges on Ashton's character discovering a list made by the titular Mr. Malcolm that enumerates all the qualities his future wife must have. She concocts a scheme to shame him for his arrogance, but real emotions begin to get in the way.

(3)   Ashton has been cast as the main villain in *Captain Marvel 2*, opposite Brie Larson. At the time of going to press, it had not been announced which character from the Marvel Comics pantheon Ashton will be portraying.

The case for
camouflage.

103   WILDEST DREAM

Photography
ROMAIN LAPRADE
Styling
GIULIA QUERENGHI

Producer
CAMILA KÖNIG
Hair & Makeup
NIKA AMBROŽIČ
Photo Assistant
POL MASIP TRULLOLS
Model
ALIOU GUEYE

(below) Aliou wears a sweater by PAUL SMITH and trousers by DAVID CATALÁN.

(below) Aliou wears a sweater by PRADA.
(right) He wears a jacket by AURALEE and trousers by DAVID CATALÁN.

THE GREAT OUTDOORS:

WORDS
Selena Takigawa Hoy
PHOTOS
Yuji Fukuhara

(THE DESIGNER)

LISA YAMAI:
Snow Peak's president wants you to get out more.

When Lisa Yamai was small, she was swept away by a river on three separate occasions. "I almost died each time, but there was always an 'outdoor person' that saved me," she says.

Yamai, who is the third-generation president of the Japanese camping and outdoor brand Snow Peak, refers to "outdoor people" a lot during our conversation. They're capable people, people who like camping, who know things about nature and how to cooperate with the land. They're the sort of people she grew up with.

Yamai is a native of Niigata, a prefecture pinned between rugged mountains and a stormy sea on the west coast of Japan's main island. It's also the location of Snow Peak headquarters, which is cradled in the foothills of Mount Awagatake to the east of Sanjo City. It's here, in the same town where her grandfather Yukio started the business all the way back in 1958, that Yamai tells me the story of Snow Peak, and its evolution into a global brand.

Yukio Yamai was a quintessential outdoor person. An avid mountain climber, he made weekly trips to Mount Tanigawa, a jagged peak straddling Niigata and Gunma Prefectures with the ominous nickname "Mountain of Death." Over 800 people have died attempting its ascent since record keeping started in 1930; by comparison, about 200 people have died in the same period on Mount Everest.

"At the time, there was no climbing gear that was appropriate for Japanese people," Yamai explains. "Rock climbing is a culture that came from the US, so gear was only suitable for Americans." Japanese climbers tended to be shorter and lither than many of their Western counterparts, and the mountains in Niigata, nicknamed "Snow Country," received upward of 30 feet of snow per winter. Yukio saw a business opportunity: "Snow Peak started making climbing gear that would accommodate Japanese people's physiques, and was geared to the mountains that they were used to climbing on a normal basis," says Yamai.

The gap in the market also allowed Yukio to combine his passion for climbing with local craft. The Tsubame-Sanjo area is famous for metalwork, and local blacksmiths have a special technique for hardening nails so as to withstand the elements. Though outdoor gear was not normally produced in local forges, Yukio negotiated with the artisans to make ice axes.

(left) Yamai wears clothing from her own eponymous label throughout.
(below) She was photographed at Snow Peak's campus in Niigata, Japan. The campus backs onto the Snow Peak Campfield—a 41-acre site used for testing gear and equipment in all weather conditions. Snow Peak has also opened a campsite in the US where outdoor enthusiasts can test their equipment before buying.

"The thought of making something for the love of nature is powerful."

Snow Peak remained dedicated to mountaineering until the 1980s, when Yukio's son Tohru Yamai came along. "Snow Peak during my grandfather's era appealed to stoic outdoor people," says Yamai. But Japan was an affluent society and flush consumers were turning toward urban pleasures. In fact, Tohru didn't initially want to be part of the company, having gone to work in Tokyo instead. His favorite way of experiencing nature was car camping—a far cry from his father's life-or-death climbs. Still, he left Tokyo's corporate life and joined the family business at around the same time that Yamai was born, in 1986.

"What my father started was a focus on enjoying nature as a family, and an outdoor style that can be enjoyed individually or as a community," says Yamai, looking out over the sprawling Snow Peak campus below, which is blooming with flowers. Tohru wanted to push back on the idea of challenging or dominating nature, focusing instead on coexisting with it. The idea coincided with the collapse of Japan's economic bubble, after which simpler pleasures became not only a romantic notion, but a necessity.

Yamai grew up steeped in camping and outdoor culture as a result. "Because the product, design and operations were all started and done by my father, I was surrounded by camping gear from the time I was born," she says. "My earliest memories are of going camping with my family on weekends to field-test the gear that my father developed."

She recalls that they often returned to a campground on Niigata's Sado Island. "I always ran around without any sense as a child, jumping into rivers like it was a normal thing." Luckily, the people in her orbit were there to pull her out, set her right, and give her the practical advice that she still remembers today as an adult.

Yamai didn't intend to join the family business either, instead pursuing fashion design in Tokyo. She quickly became disillusioned. "In the Tokyo fashion world, people are chased by their work and lose their humanity," she says. "I thought, I was reared in an environment surrounded by nature, and I want to do work that takes advantage of that."

As the president of Snow Peak, she has added an apparel division to the company, bringing together two worlds that had little—and wanted even less—to do with one another. Fashion may seem an odd ancillary in the outdoor realm, which traditionally has valued function over form, but Yamai's urban aesthetic and outdoorsy background have helped forge the brand's modern image.

Under her influence, Snow Peak's designs are a departure from the prevailing trends at other outdoor brands, which favor bold blocks of often primary colors in '90s silhouettes. In contrast, Snow Peak's clothes come in beige, gray and dun tones, and are often loose or drapey, with rough textures and intricate details. Although you'll find high-tech, lightweight fabrics including nylon and polyester, Snow Peak also uses materials like yak and alpaca wool, along with organic cotton. A number of bestsellers take cues from Japanese culture and fashion, such as the fire-resistant Takibi line, based on Japanese firefighter gear, and the Dotera and Noragi jackets, which both nod to the kimono.

With her own fashion brand, Yamai, which is independent from Snow Peak, she channels inspiration from nature into designs intended for urban environments. The Yamai brand uses delicate fabrics that originate in nature: She gestures to her own outfit, which she tells me is made from Indian wild silk. "I have a strong desire to create clothing that has wilderness endowed within it," she says. "And the thought of making something for the love of nature is powerful." This is what she wants for Snow Peak too: "The idea is to create functions and designs that blend into nature."

Most people, Yamai thinks, are woefully disconnected from the outdoors. "People are part of nature, and people's lives are intertwined closely with nature. But people don't want to inconvenience themselves. They don't want to get wet in the rain," she says. The more disconnected people become from the elements, the less likely they are to care about environmental impacts, for example, or the question of where their food comes from. Yamai recalls a trip to Western Mongolia, where she lived in a ger with nomads for a weekend. She came away impressed by their cooperation with the land. She sees her role as bringing people and nature closer together, even in the city. Yamai hopes that by attracting stylish urbanites to camping, they might become more attuned to their consumption, where those resources come from and what remains.

"Ever since fast fashion came about in the industry, mass production and consumption have been extremely burdensome to the environment," says Yamai. "Rather than making clothing that serves capitalist economic thinking, I want to get as close to traceability as I can manage. I want the clothing to make you feel close to nature, to make you think about nature," she explains. "We have to live in humility toward nature."

(right)   Yamai is the third-generation president of Snow Peak. Under her grandfather, the brand was for mountaineers. Her father shifted the emphasis to car camping and coexisting with nature. Yamai has introduced apparel that allows the wearer to transition seamlessly between urban and outdoor environments.

The Dutch designer bringing life—and death—to traditional gardens.

(THE GARDENER)

PIET

OUDOLF

WORDS
Alice Vincent
PHOTOS
Marina Denisova

Over the past four decades, one man has steadily changed the way our parks and gardens feel. Piet Oudolf is a Dutch designer who cut through the prim fussiness of traditional Western gardens with an unapologetic determination to make our green spaces seem more alive. There's a good chance you've admired an Oudolf garden without realizing it. Perhaps you are one of the eight million people who visit Manhattan's elevated park, the High Line, every year, or maybe you visited his riotous meadow inside the 2011 Serpentine Pavilion in London or the Oudolf Garten at the Vitra campus in Weil am Rhein, Germany, which opened to the public last year.

His is a language of swaying, fluffy grasses and tactile outcrops of woodland foliage; a shift from gaudy, disposable bedding plants to something altogether more natural. Through plants, he conjures strange and beautiful dreamscapes.

Oudolf is 78 and still working, but he's wrangling with "winding down." The first meeting he had with the landscape architects behind the High Line was in 2004, and he's still involved. "It evolves constantly, so it's a constant process of making little changes so that it can evolve in the right way," he explains. He is a designer contemplating the end of a career. With it, comes a question: What legacy can be left by an artist whose creations have always prioritized experience over permanence?

An online search for "Hummelo" will bring up a variety of *Stachys* that Oudolf has developed, but it's also a town 75 miles east of Amsterdam, and Oudolf's home of 40 years. On a Zoom call from his home studio, he appears in a red flannel shirt over a white T-shirt, a strand of white hair falling down the side of his face. He wears the tan—and the frown lines—of a man who has spent five

decades outside, but it's still difficult to believe that Oudolf is nearly 80. He is businesslike and serious but not without warmth. His studio is a spacious white box of a room that holds a table and, beneath the windows that look out over the garden, shelving for the neat rolls of paper he uses for the large designs he draws out by hand.

He works here alone, currently switching between eight to 10 projects. For each, Oudolf collaborates with what he calls a "network" of people—landscape architects, contractors, planting specialists—but it is on the long table behind him where the gardens start, with tracing paper and colored Sharpies, as he spends weeks mapping out intricate patterns of symbols and letters that will become moving, growing plant matter.

Oudolf moved here from the Haarlem suburbs in 1982 with his wife, Anja, and their two small children. It was a derelict farmhouse. At the time, he was a freelance garden designer, having found work in a garden center after leaving his family restaurant and trying on different professional hats with little success. "I sort of got lost into plants," he says. "But I felt stuck in my progress. We made nice gardens but it was too small. I had the feeling that I could do more and especially with plants, that instead of designing we had to grow plants."

"Grow plants" is a modest descriptor of the nursery that the couple created over 1½ acres. Hummelo became a holy grail of progressive horticulturalists, filled with meticulously sourced and developed varieties that simply weren't brought together elsewhere. Decades on, and Oudolf creations such as the effervescent *Gaura lindheimeri* "Whirling Butterflies" or the striking *Salvia verticillata* "Purple Rain" have become regular bed-fillers in discerning domestic gardens.

> "No garden lives forever. We are not creating nature, we make gardens."

There was a fierce philosophy beneath the aesthetics. Oudolf became friends with Henk Gerritsen, an ecologist-turned-garden designer known for pioneering the "Dutch Wave," a horticultural movement determined to do things differently. "His work was wild," says Oudolf, who had trained in the rigors of English gardening, a near-omnipresent tradition that defied geographical borders. "I came from the world of English gardening and he came from wild gardening and we met each other in thinking about how gardens should be. The whole conversation was about how we could do gardens differently. We started to talk about spontaneity."

Gerritsen lived with HIV until 2009 and, in the mid-1990s, lost his partner to AIDs-related illness. He encouraged Oudolf to see the vitality of death in a garden. "He pointed out the beauty of plants after flowering," Oudolf says. "He showed me, in the garden, the processes of what happens if you let things go." This is a crucial part of any Oudolf garden—the letting go. I saw it in the Oudolf Field in Bruton, England, one bright October day: The blackened heads of globe thistles and Echinacea punctuated feathered grasses as asters rustled in the breeze. It was dying, and unbelievably beautiful. "People try to cut back everything after it has flowered, but you lose a lot of depth or interest and beauty that way," he says.

Together, in 1992, Gerritsen and Oudolf published *Droomplanten*, or Dream Plants, a compendium of 1,200 perennial plants "that were very good garden plants but never used because they were just wild in other people's eyes," Oudolf says. "We wrote about plants that had good skeletons or seed heads." He still deploys many of them in his work three decades on.

Over the years, some people have seen Oudolf as something of a Gerritsen protégé, and he's keen to establish that wasn't the case. "It's not that I took over from other people's vision," he says. "I had a very strong idea about what I wanted, but it was fed by his input."

In 2000, Oudolf debuted at London's RHS Chelsea Flower Show with British garden designer Arne Maynard. Amid a sea of glossy new millennium water features, their Evolution garden presented a moody foliage palette and cloud-pruned box hedging. They won best in show; elements of their design can be traced through many of the Chelsea show gardens that have been built since.

127

The accolades and industry prowess, though, drift away when actually standing in an Oudolf garden. I remember visiting the High Line for the first time in 2010, when I had no idea what either the High Line or an Oudolf design was. It was late afternoon in early September, eggy sun splintering off the Hudson River and through long grasses. When I returned, in 2017, there was more: woodland areas and small meadows. It felt impossible that this existed here above New York City sidewalks. These colors, these structures, all these little lives and deaths on display.

"Gardens are sort of a conversation without speaking," Oudolf says. "I think what we do [as designers] is send out a message—of life, of how you feel, of how you could feel. What I see, I try to let people see as well." He sees his work as "falling in love with the small things and bringing them together to make a big thing." Those small things, he later lists off, include "the seasonality, the moment in time, the context, the combination. It's what it does to you."

When Oudolf talks about plants—using them, designing with them, being among them—he often compares them to music, or food. At one point, he compares the nuance of his designs to "tasting different layers instead of just, 'this is sauerkraut' or 'this is vegetable soup.'" There's a sense that they're sometimes just a medium, like paint or a piano, that facilitates his creativity. Developing the nursery at Hummelo, he tells me, "made me feel that I could express myself and my inner feelings by doing this. It came to me sort of suddenly, within months, and it never left me."

"He's driven by a need to create," says Thomas Piper, a filmmaker who followed Oudolf for his documentary *Five Seasons: The Gardens of Piet Oudolf*. "My favorite comment I hear from people after they have seen the movie is, 'I look at the world completely differently now.' That's what Piet does with his gardens. He changes the way we see."

Oudolf has always been aware of the ephemerality of his work. Most of his designs, such as that at Wisley in England, which he's currently reworking, have a lifespan of 20 years. After that, the natural evolution of the plants means it is unrecognizable from the garden he designed. "You lose things and you win things and I think sometimes you have to change it." They exist longer on paper than they do on the ground. Perhaps his most concrete creative inheritance is the designs that can be downloaded from his website. Next year, Phaidon will publish all of them in a book. "I give it away so that if you need to know how to do it you can," he says. "I have built gardens, and no garden that I can see lives forever. We are not creating nature, we make gardens. I think we try to do something that is for the time we live in and the context we live in. Everything has the complexity of time where you build it."

I ask him about legacy, whether he cares about it. "No," he replies, "the fact is that you get better all the time. Your ideas get stronger, your designs get stronger." Some of the gardens he made 20 years ago would not be to his taste now, he says, but he recognizes that it was the product of that era. Oudolf decided last winter not to take on any new projects that would last longer than three years. Anja, who has worked alongside him for decades, is "doing less."

And yet, there's still what he calls a "force"—a creative urge, a need to keep pushing different combinations of plants, to capture different feelings. "I still try to keep up with how I feel, and how I can make it better or different. Not easy," he pauses, cracking the smallest of smiles, "but that's how I feel it."

"Gardens are a conversation without speaking. What I see, I try to let people see as well."

THE GREAT OUTDOORS

GABE VERDUZCO: A microscopic tour of California's beetles and botanicals.

WORDS Stephanie d'Arc Taylor   PHOTOS Justin Chung

The platonic ideal of a park ranger—a rugged outdoors type most at home in wild places—infrequently corresponds with the reality of the underpaid, beleaguered government employees working the information desks at America's state parks. Gabe Verduzco, however, is an exception.

Having loved plants since he was a kid in California's fertile Central Valley, Verduzco now devotes his professional and personal life to maintaining and protecting the native trees, flowers and fauna of Southern California. One recent Friday morning, Verduzco brought Stephanie d'Arc Taylor on a tour of the South Coast Botanic Garden in Palos Verdes and chatted with her as he surveyed native trees for evidence of invasive pests.

STEPHANIE D'ARC TAYLOR: How did you first get interested in plants?

GABE VERDUZCO: I grew up in the agricultural heart of California, and I always had a thing for being outside. Right behind our house were fields of grapes, down the street were plum trees. There were fruit trees growing everywhere. I just loved being outdoors, but particularly in nature. Even when I was playing baseball as a kid, I would be standing out there, not paying attention to the game but looking at the butterflies.

SDT: What was the first thing you ever planted for yourself?

GV: I started vegetable gardening at a young age. We always liked carving pumpkins, and one day I just had the idea, I'm gonna try and plant this and grow it. That was the first thing I ever planted. I was probably 12 or 13. The funny thing is that my mom ended up pulling it out because she thought it was a weed.

SDT: Tell me about your day job.

GV: My full-time job is with the University of California, Agricultural and Natural Resources division. We work with invasive tree pests, specifically the invasive shot hole borer beetle, gold spotted oak borer beetle and Asian citrus psyllid. I'm also a part-time park ranger at Dana Point Nature Reserve and I manage the social media account for the Orange County chapter of the

"When I was playing baseball, I'd be looking at the butterflies."

California Native Plant Society. And I try to surf at least once a day!

SDT: What's a day in your life like?

GV: I'll spend my days in parks or wilderness areas surveying plants and trees for invasive pests. It's great because I can spot native flowers or plants or critters and share them on my Instagram account. I mean, I'm still being efficient with my work, but if I see something beautiful I'll take a picture and educate myself about it. Some of the parks have a lot of transient folks living there, which can be tricky. Also when we have to survey wilderness zones, we're deep in the thick of it with snakes, spiders. We wear snake guards because we've come across rattlesnakes for sure.

SDT: [Pointing] Here's a sycamore, let's check for beetles! What do you look for when you approach a tree?

GV: So when I approach a tree, I'll look at it from a distance and examine it. If you look at this branch over here, you can see that it did have a shot hole beetle infestation at one point and it might still have it. Look at these welts and tiny holes. That's where the beetle once dug into it. The beetle produces a fungus that prevents nutrients from reaching the leaves, which is what ultimately can kill a tree. But the tree can fight it off as well. See these warty bits that look like welts? We'd call this callusing or compartmentalizing; it shows that the tree is trying to fight it off. Maybe a year or two ago I would have mentioned something to the garden management, but at this point, the tree has been able to fight it off and heal. I think it's going to be okay.

SDT: Such drama! Tell me more about how a tree fights off a beetle infestation.

GV: Imagine there's a group of people and we all get COVID. We're all going to react differently—one could get sick, one could be asymptomatic. It's similar to trees. One tree could die because it doesn't have the ability to fight the beetle off as well, but these other sycamores have more immunity. If one tree gets an infestation there's a way they communicate so others can mount their defenses. This tree is probably close to 100 years old. We've been losing trees at this scale. Trees like this provide shade, beautify the spaces, clean the air and provide wildlife habitat. You can hear the birdsong now. Birds, butterflies, hummingbirds: It's a whole ecosystem that we want to protect.

A scholar
at one
with the
elements.

AYANA

WORDS
Sala Elise Patterson
PHOTOS
Ted Belton

When archaeologist Ayana Omilade Flewellen is excavating a site, they are in pursuit not only of artifacts but also of signs of humanity. More precisely, they are looking for physical evidence left by enslaved Africans and their descendants of lives lived, love bestowed and fates crushed or graced with good fortune. For Flewellen, an assistant professor of archaeology at Stanford University, retrieving that evidence is about more than archaeological discovery. It is an exercise in dismantling dominant narratives about Black people in the United States. At former slave plantations, or in waters off the US Virgin Islands, their work holds up these fragments of the past and presents them as a challenge: *Claim the hurt you have inflicted, confront the humanity whose existence you had to deny in order to enslave an entire people.*

"As a Black nonbinary archaeologist who first and foremost centers Black life in my work, when doing archaeological work on sites of enslavement or freedom post-1865 in the United States, it becomes important to describe Black life and Black humanity, because in the past, African descendant people have been treated like chattel and have been quantified and abstracted to the quantifiable," Flewellen explains, speaking from their mother's home in Michigan.

Flewellen's research focuses on exploring sites along the extended path traveled by Africans brought to America in chains. This means excavating at former plantations in the lush landscapes of the American South but also in the waters of the Caribbean, exploring the wreckage of sunken slave ships, which some estimates place at more than 1,000. As a child, they grew up snorkeling in the waters off Miami, but needed scuba dive training to be able to excavate on the ocean floor.

"I've always been drawn to water in the way that you spend all day at a beach. But never in my life had I thought about scuba diving until 2015," they recall. The training was vital: "It's one thing to carry your trowel, measuring tape, and shovel on land. It is something entirely different to have all of the measuring equipment you need underwater and keep things streamlined while you float with all of your gear, making sure not to damage the wreck or the sea life around you."

Their first dive to a vessel used in the transatlantic slave trade was to the wreckage of The Clotilda, a ship that carried more than 100 Africans to Alabama in 1860, 52 years after the importation of enslaved people was banned. This expedition was thus carried out in secret, and upon arrival the ship was sunk to hide evidence of the (double) crime. Flewellen recalls what they found: "The Clotilda is the most intact vessel that we have access to today and part of that is because oftentimes wrecking events will quite literally tear these ships apart. So your wreck site is sprawled out over several hundred feet. But, because this wreck was done in a clandestine manner, the majority of the ship was intact. And because of that, it presents this real, tangible history, an acknowledgment of some of the most horrible aspects of the transatlantic slave trade, which is the actual space of confinement in the hull itself."

Today, Flewellen is on the board of Diving with a Purpose, a nonprofit dedicated to oceanic conservation and the preservation of submerged heritage resources, and spends a lot of time in breathtaking waters. In fact, the formidable beauty of their dig locations on land and water sits in striking contrast to the horrors that took place there. That juxtaposition is not lost on Flewellen, nor is the salve that nature provides for work that can, at times, weigh heavy on the soul. "The great outdoors for me feels like freedom, the great escape. My work quite literally allows me to connect with land, soil and water in ways that remind me of the importance and interconnection of nature in our everyday lives."

But what really buoys Flewellen is the material culture they encounter. Those objects become fodder for their entire body of work, from devising new narratives, to analyzing the world we have inherited from history, to inspiring their visual art in the form of sculpture, collage and performance. Sometimes, an object will speak to bigger truths. Take, for example, a discovery made while researching their current book on clothing and adornment practices among African American women between 1865 to 1900: "I was looking at a collection from the site of a Black land-owning family in Texas dating from 1871. There were small shoe soles and hooks used to button shoes, which I imagine were used by children. During enslavement, the rationing of clothing was so severe that people often had one or two pairs of trousers or shirts to last the entire year. Oftentimes children went without shoes. So, there's something about those shoe soles and button hooks for children that speaks to a desire that Black families had, and access Black families had post-emancipation to build a different kind of life."

And it is here that Flewellen blows past the science of archaeology, anthropology and history into a colorful expanse of intimate knowing "as a storyteller and as an artist operating through a Black feminist framework." Their whole person pours through the work.

"Never in my life had I thought about scuba diving."

(above)   To descend to great depths while diving, Flewellen uses lead weights to help them sink through the salt water.

146   THE GREAT OUTDOORS

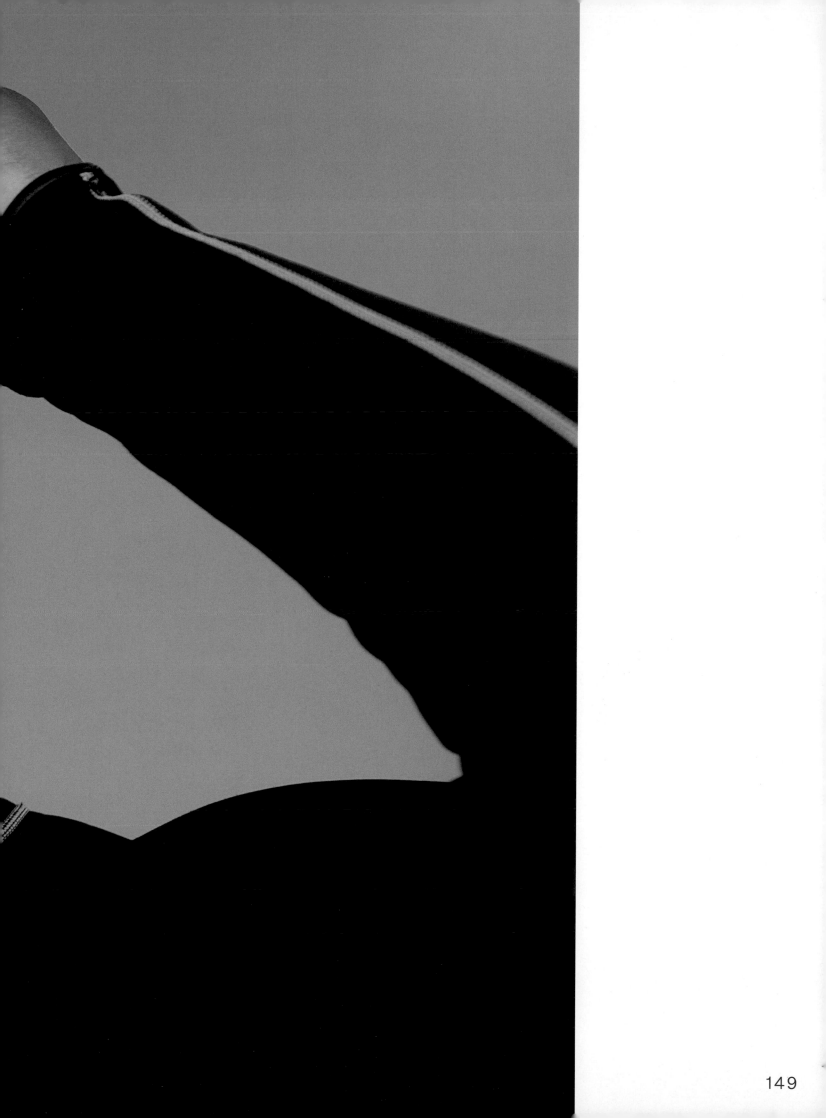

(THE REWILDER)

THOMAS MACDONELL:
The conservationist transforming the Highlands.

WORDS Harriet Fitch Little   PHOTOS Richard Gaston

" I know now that there's a lag before the habitat responds."

the reason why so little grows: The tender pine has had most of its branches bitten off. "Red deer," he says, and looks displeased.[1] Across the Highlands, this is what the deer are doing: ravaging the land like slugs might a vegetable patch. What's left is a monoculture of heather, which thrives in unshaded soil, and the uniform, ecologically uninteresting timber forests that are protected by fencing during their early growth.

MacDonell doesn't blame the deer. "It's mismanagement by humans that has allowed them to become the enemy," he explains. "We've removed wolves, and we've removed lynx from the environment, so we don't have apex predators." Shooting estates, which are a mainstay of the Highlands' economy, don't help; guests want to shoot mature stags rather than the females, and the blood sport industry is very resistant to culls.

Since the deer came to dominate the Highlands, biodiversity, soil structure and habitats for birds and small mammals have all suffered. Even the deer are struggling because of the lack of trees: "It wasn't unusual to have 200 deer lying dead in the snow because they couldn't get into woodland for shelter," recalls MacDonell, who grew up locally and speaks with the authority of someone who has learned their trade through talking, observing and doing, rather than from formal study.

"Rewilding" is a fashionable word and conjures images of a gentle process; leaving a lawn unmown perhaps, or scattering some wildflower seed and letting nature do its thing. This is nothing like what MacDonell is doing. His process is interventionist, you might almost say industrial. Since 2006, he has directed his team to fell 300 hectares of non-native lodgepole pine timber forests, cut new roads and—most drastically—kill thousands of deer in an attempt to reduce the population density from 50 per square kilometer to two so as to reduce the pressure from grazing.

He admits now that it was a big swing. "We went through a period of having shot thousands of deer and nothing was responding. That was a lonely period," he recalls. Then, after four long years, pine seedlings appeared amid the scrubby grass and heather shrubs. MacDonell had been vindicated. With the benefit of hindsight, he says, "I know now that there's a lag before the habitat responds."

MacDonell drives me to Glenfeshie, the Wildland estate that is furthest along in the process of rewilding. It is, to the Highlands, what an oasis is to the desert. The hillside track meanders through lush, varied woodland that has sprung up naturally from blown-in seed (although in very barren areas

Visitors to Scotland's Highlands have always liked to imagine that they are traveling through a landscape untouched by human hands. Here, at the northernmost tip of the United Kingdom, there are more red deer than residents and it is not unusual for a trip to the nearest supermarket to take the best part of a day. The countryside is vast and brutal, with peat bogs, freezing lochs and bare mountains reaching up to a sky that always threatens rain. This is a place where few plants grow taller than the scrubby, ubiquitous heather; where even day hikers can feel they are doing well just to survive.

The only problem with this romantic vision of desolation is that it's a fantasy. In May, I traveled to the Cairngorms National Park to spend the day with Thomas Mac-Donell, director of conservation at Wildland, a conglomerate of estates in the Highlands owned by Danish billionaire Anders Holch Povlsen. At 220,000 acres, Wildland is the largest private land holding in the United Kingdom. If Povlsen and MacDonell have their way, it will also be the most radical: They want to "rewild" this portion of the Highlands, recreating a natural landscape not seen for centuries.

As we bump along dirt tracks in Mac-Donell's four-by-four, he makes short work of destroying the popular perception of this region as naturally barren. Trees *should* grow here, MacDonell says—Scots pines, silver birch and rowan trees should flank the hillsides, alders should carpet the river banks, with wild roses and raspberries winding up through them. There should be bird cherry trees, bilberries and meadows full of cotton grass, their pom-pom-like seed heads carpeting the landscape like snow.

High on a hillside, MacDonell jumps down from the car into the drizzle and points to a knee-high sapling that demonstrates

---

(1)   MacDonell analyzes sapling damage like a detective might a crime scene. A clean cut across a branch at 90 degrees indicates that it has been eaten by a red deer. Hares, by comparison, leave a clean cut at 45 degrees, while roe deer pull the bark off as they bite.

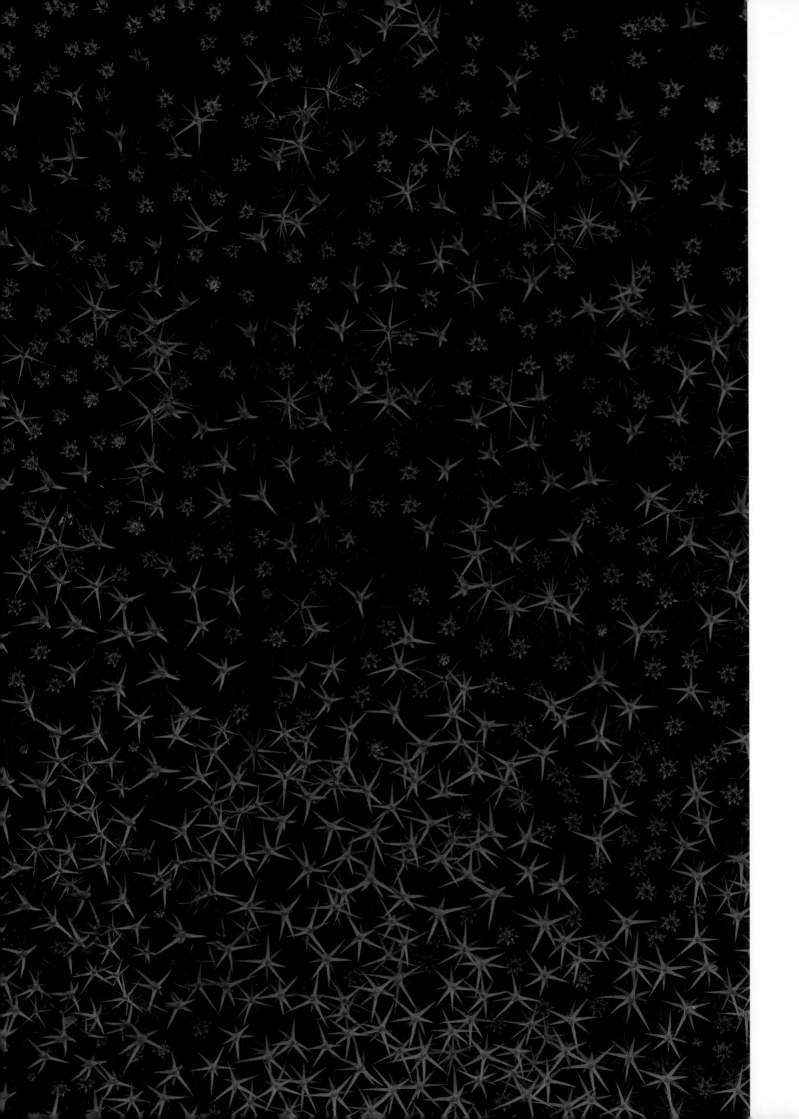

MacDonell has planted saplings in formations that mimic the natural rhythms of the woodland). Some saplings have reached almost four meters, and they crowd the track on either side. A rare black grouse pokes its head up on a hillside nearby. MacDonell tells me he's actually looking forward to the day when deer can return in greater numbers and cut some paths through the thick growth. "They are the natural sculptors [of the woodland], not the enemy," he says.

We descend into the valley and ford a river, then continue on foot along the banks, where MacDonell outlines a very complicated, domino-effect plan to encourage salmon to build redds, or nests, in the river by encouraging tree growth along the riverside. It will be 15 years before he'll know if it's working, which makes this one of the shorter-term projects he's undertaking; Wildland's media strategy centers on the idea of a 200-year vision for regeneration. Really, MacDonell admits, it should be 300 years—which is the life of a pine tree—but he tells me, po-faced, that 200 years sounds "a little bit more here and now."

MacDonell trained as an engineer, which he says has made him a pragmatic conservationist. Unlike some starry, nostalgic initiatives, Wildland isn't trying to turn back the clocks to a pre-human age; in fact, MacDonell himself owns a croft (a small farm) with cows and sheep, and his decisions are informed by an agricultural perspective. It's the reason he's hesitant about reintroducing wolves and lynx in Scotland, an idea that gets tossed about with some regularity. "I would be one of the people who would probably lose a few of my 30 sheep," he says. "I'm trying to be consistent with my own experiences."[2]

MacDonell is also matter-of-fact when talking about the impact that Povlsen's enormous wealth has had on Wildland. "If I got gifted Glenfeshie Estate, I wouldn't have had the resources to do this," he says. Because of the huge investment needed to kick-start the process of rewilding, the estate is currently operating with a £3 million net loss every year. "That's the argument I have in my mind for wealthy people owning land." Povlsen is not the only ecologically minded foreigner buying land in the Highlands; in fact, the phenomenon has become so recognized that the media has christened them "green lairds"—laird being the traditional honorific for a Scottish landowner. "It doesn't really matter where they come from, it's more about what they do when they're here," he says.

After leaving MacDonell, I drive the three-hour road from the Cairngorms to Tongue, a tiny hamlet overlooking a narrow arm of water leading out into the North Sea. Here, surrounded by land also owned by Povlsen, I stay at Lundies House—one of the hotels that Wildland hopes will provide long-term income for the rewilding project.

It is a small and extraordinarily beautiful property, with a scrubbed stone exterior and art-filled rooms that mimic the layout of a particularly rich and comfortable home. MacDonell had joked during our conversation that the rough-and-ready Scottish countryside wasn't always a natural fit for Danes, with their tendency toward tidiness. At Lundies House, however, it seems the two styles fit very well. The hotel has eschewed the tartan detailing that is so often used as a signifier of the Highlands, but there are oversized vases in every room bursting with flowering broom, birch branches and even young nettles, grounding the house in its wild surroundings.

The Tongue estate is only a few years into its rewilding process, and the landscape has none of the lush vegetation of Glenfeshie. Walking up to the summit of Ben Tongue, a small mountain that looks over the village, I flatten wet heather with every step. Looking inland, the landscape is unbroken; low, rolling mountains in brown and yellow extend as far as the eye can see. It is Scotland at its most epic—and barren. I can't pretend I don't think it's stunning. But soon there will be trees here, and then birds, flowers, berries and insects wriggling their way up through the nourished soil. As with human beauty, the standards by which we evaluate a landscape can evolve. In the Highlands, they must.

(2) MacDonell has also decided not to remove non-native tree species that pose no risk to local plants, such as the sycamore (brought over from France in the Middle Ages). And he has kept some of the planted pine forests because they provide an important habitat for the capercaillie, a turkey-sized grouse threatened with extinction. Only once the new woodland has grown to a point where it can provide a habitat for the capercaillie would MacDonell consider removing these plantations.

" I'm trying to
be consistent
with my own
experiences."

EL
LA

The scientist digging for history in the world's most hostile landscapes.

(THE EXPLORER)

WORDS
Tom Faber
PHOTOS
Rick Pushinsky

You might think, with every inch of the earth's surface meticulously charted and the whole store of human knowledge available on the internet, that there is no place in the 21st century for explorers. Scientist and TV host Ella Al-Shamahi, who was named a National Geographic Emerging Explorer in 2015, thinks otherwise—she feels we simply need to update our understanding of what it means to be an explorer today.

Al-Shamahi specializes in archaeological digs across the world's most politically unstable and hostile territories, where scientific institutions often fear to tread. These regions include pivotal sites of early human history. By ignoring them, Al-Shamahi believes we're missing a huge part of our own story.

Born to Yemeni parents in Birmingham, England, Al-Shamahi believed in creationism growing up. At university, she attempted to disprove Darwin's theory of evolution—a fact which now causes her great embarrassment. On finding the evidence for evolution surprisingly robust, she had a change of heart and decided to dedicate her life to the study of early humans, specializing in Neanderthals.

Al-Shamahi has a second life as a stand-up comic, where she incorporates scientific research into her act. Her combination of academic approachability and easy charisma has led her to host TV shows on subjects including the Indigenous people of the Amazon, the boy pharaoh Tutankhamun and the lives of Viking women for the BBC, PBS, National Geographic and the Discovery Channel.

TOM FABER: Why is it important to do scientific research in politically unstable areas?

ELLA AL-SHAMAHI: It's a tragedy for those places if we ignore them. It's also, quite selfishly, a tragedy for science. Realistically, that's where we're going to make the next big discoveries— it's already happening in places like the rain forests.

TF: What extra hurdles are there to overcome when you do fieldwork in hostile territories?

Hair & Makeup: Jinny Kim.

EAS: It's exhausting to organize even a normal expedition—you've got to generate funding, assemble teams and work out the logistics behind the science. In addition, you've got to jump through the biggest hoops with regards to security, safety and politics. I once worked in a highly disputed territory where we didn't even know who to ask for permission to work there. We were literally looking at UN documents trying to work out whose jurisdiction it was. Then when we arrived back from our dig in the mountains, we were told that we had just been working in a minefield.

TF: How do you prepare for your research trips?

EAS: I'm lucky that, because of my Arabic background, I was aware of a lot of political stuff anyway. I remember on childhood trips to Yemen we learned that certain people in our group shouldn't speak because their accent reveals they come from a certain region or that they're Western. I had to learn to walk differently—you can sometimes identify a Western woman by the way we walk with fewer constraints, like we own the place. I change the way I walk, the way I talk, the way I carry myself. You're trying to camouflage and blend in. I make my curly hair look different in different places.

TF: Despite all the challenges, do you think we have an obligation to conduct research in such places?

EAS: My argument isn't that everybody should go work in these places. My argument is that if my mates can work in very dangerous underground caves, or with poisonous snakes or in dangerous ocean conditions as long as they've gone through the appropriate training, then why are we told we're not allowed to work in disputed territories by funding bodies?

TF: We don't use the term "explorer" much these days. It almost feels antiquated. How do you relate to the label?

EAS: If *National Geographic* hadn't called me an explorer, I would never use the term. It's weird to use it without that context. But when I talk to kids, I say that when I imagined an explorer when I was younger, it was a rich white man from a different century with a big beard covered in snow. So I get a glint in my eyes when I'm described as an explorer because it's so subversive. There's a lot left to be explored but we need a different kind of exploration: more responsible and humane. I'd like to think we don't use phrases like "this is the first" unless it really is the first, that we don't feel ownership. In my field I see a lot of people who think they own a place because they've done a bit of work there and I'm like: No you don't, that's really weird and super colonial.

TF: Do you think we can move past the colonial overtones of the word "explorer" and keep using it?

"We need a different kind of exploration: more responsible and humane."

(right)   Al-Shamahi was photographed at Chelsea Physic Garden in London—one of the oldest botanical gardens in Europe.

EAS: For me, it's a bit like *Indiana Jones*. The films are a lot of fun; I'll happily watch them. But they're completely sexist and there are shades of colonialism. Also there's just bad science: He never even uses a trowel. And who brings a whip onto an archaeological site? But at the same time, he has introduced the masses to archaeology. The best PR archaeology has had in the last 50 years is *Indiana Jones*. I rarely see the point of throwing the baby out with the bathwater. Instead I prefer shifting terms, getting people to think about how we're using them instead of just throwing it all out.

TF: What are you actually doing day-to-day when you're on an expedition?

EAS: It depends. TV expeditions are completely different—they're not real. A real expedition is bloody hardcore. Generally, it's a lot of logistics, walking landscapes for ages trying to find the caves, and then it's bog-standard archaeology—get your square and dig in it.

TF: I imagine it's hard to make a TV show out of that.

EAS: That's why it's rare that a TV show is built around just one dig. They're usually built around a thesis or journey that covers multiple digs. Ceramics or stone tools are very important for scientific knowledge but they don't always translate onto the screen. The audience is more interested in your broad conclusions from that dig. I mean, I love looking at bits of Neanderthal teeth because I understand their context, but the general public is looking at it going: "It's a tooth, mate, it's a tooth. Why are you so excited?"

TF: Do you feel an emotional connection to fossils and Neanderthal teeth?

EAS: Yeah, I do. It's bizarre, but now is the only time on our planet where only one species of human has existed. Before, we were sharing the planet with multiple other species of human. There's an obvious fascination with them. What happened to them? What was it like for that last Neanderthal? Did he or she know that they were the last? We interbred with Neanderthals and I can't help but wonder what that looked like—were they normal unions or were they controversial for their people?

TF: Do you feel a sense of responsibility?

EAS: Constantly. I live in a permanent state of anxiety because of it. I know how unusual it is for a woman of color to have my job and I have a responsibility to make sure that the messaging of my shows is correct, all while ensuring the science is accurate and maintaining a bit of storytelling. It's a headache.

TF: Does that responsibility extend to the local people in the unstable areas where you work? What does it mean for them when fossils are discovered?

EAS: In some places I work, like Yemen or Iraq, people have a strong sense of pride but feel really forgotten by the world. So they start noticing: "Oh, our place is useful for this kind of fossil? So we're important to the human story, are we?" And I'm like: Yes! Of course you are!

"I get a glint in my eyes when I'm described as an explorer because it's so subversive."

(left)   Chelsea Physic Garden's plant collection is unique in being the only botanic garden collection focused on medicinal, herbal and useful plants.

CΛRA MΛRIE PIAZZA: The New Yorker wringing color from the city's waste and weeds.

WORDS Rosalind Jana   PHOTOS Emma Trim

Cara Marie Piazza's studio in East Williamsburg, Brooklyn, is a plant-lover's paradise. When we speak over Zoom, she is framed by piles of foliage on the table behind her and dried sprigs of barberry hanging on the wall. When she gesticulates, the ends of her fingers form fans of inky blue. Piazza is a natural dyer and artist, which means she takes her pigments from the world around her. From the time that she first dyed a silk slip 12 years ago, she's been enchanted by the alchemic possibilities of plants, botanicals, clays and nontoxic metals. Piazza first discovered the medium when she was studying at London's Chelsea College of Art and Design. There she took a workshop on dyeing with onion skins. "That's where the seed was planted, forgive the pun," she recalls.

These days Piazza sources her materials from all over. Food waste comes from restaurants, and herbs and weeds from New York's hidden corners. She also partners with local farms, including the North Fork Flower Farm, as well as working with florists and composting services to create dyes from the leftover floral arrangements at weddings and fashion week events. Piazza herself is becoming something of a fashion favorite too, having collaborated with designers including Jason Wu and Mara Hoffman.

ROSALIND JANA: Why natural dyes? What's the appeal?

CARA MARIE PIAZZA: Besides it being a craft that is more sustainable—I think that word gets thrown around too much—there is this sense of creative exploration and play that happens in working with natural dyes. The mystery and the surprise draws me to it every time. Also, time in New York is a precious commodity. So having to work with the plants in a way that is slow and considered and not rushed is such a welcome respite from the busy world that surrounds me.

RJ: That idea of "play" makes me think about the childish, elemental pleasure of mixing flowers in water to create an amazing smell, or to watch the colors transform.

CMP: There is this magic as a kid—the innocence of being able to gather leaves and make potions and let your imagination run wild. That |still| happens for me every time I create a

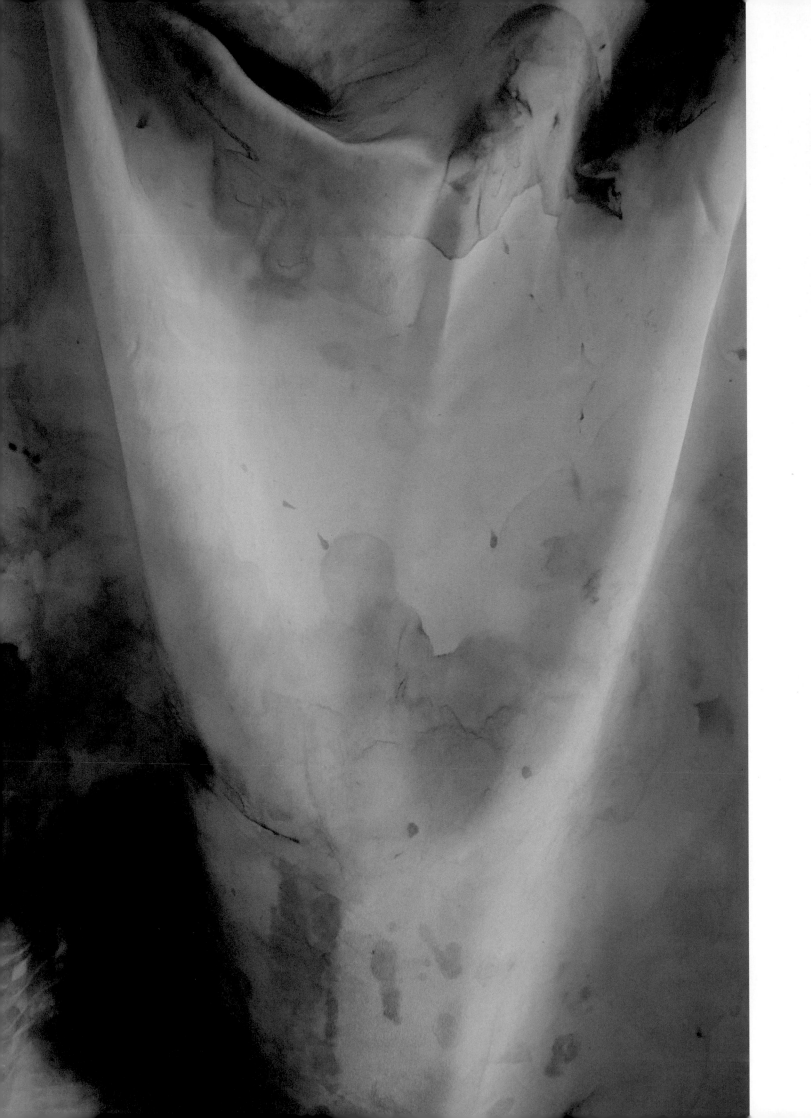

recipe. As adults, we're often taught that there needs to be a monetary value attached to that at the end. I hope that for the people who take my classes, they're able to practice and just play. It offers you a chance to pause, reevaluate and reimagine the ways that you connect with nature.

RJ: Do you ever go foraging for materials yourself?

CMP: My favorite foraging comes from New York City. As a New Yorker, I think that often the natural world is overlooked. But if you look closely, it's everywhere. You have to be careful where you forage, because you want to be mindful of not taking something that was sprayed with pesticides, but a lot of flowers and plants that would typically be deemed as invasive or weeds make great dyes. Herbs as well. Mugwort is an amazing one. Goldenrod too. I try to work with plant matter that might be a nuisance to someone else. Natural dyes are extracts. If you're not harvesting responsibly, you're still being extractive.... Working in a way where we're taking something that's overabundant, something that someone else might think is quite annoying, that excites me.

RJ: You're vocal about the importance of green spaces in urban settings. I take it you're not running away to the middle of nowhere anytime soon?

CMP: It's a mix. That's the joke of being a New Yorker: You need to leave to want to come back. I'm at peace when I'm in places like the North Fork of Long Island where I have the Sound and the beach and the farmland. I call it the little Mediterranean. But I would be lying if I said that I didn't also get a lot of my energy from the pulse of New York. I feel like more plant people need to come and re-green the city. I want to bring more nature in. There are so many opportunities for community gardens, rooftop gardens—just using the little space you have on your fire escape to grow herbs.

RJ: You've worked with designers including Jason Wu and Mara Hoffman. How do those collaborations fit into your wider work?

CMP: They've been amazing. For Jason Wu, it was a different process because I created digital prints. I didn't physically hand dye. At first, I was a bit worried about working in that way, because I felt like it wasn't as sustainable. But the truth is, digital print uses no water. You can't be 100% pure, it's impossible. Working with Mara [Hoffman] was incredible. For our first collaboration after COVID, she was sitting on all this inventory, and wasn't sure what to do with it. She came to me, and we dyed this capsule [collection]. It was an amazing confluence of events where we turned something that could have been potentially wasteful into a great silver lining.

RJ: It must be exciting for a commercial label to have the opportunity to create one-of-a-kind garments.

CMP: That's the beauty of it. It's like an artist's edition, right? There'll be a set of 50 or 100 that all are a little bit off and unique, but they locate you to that place and time that they were made. Me and my studio manager, Erin, work on everything, just the two of us. We've got our hands on every single garment or textile.

RJ: Has it made you rethink your relationship with color? When you're out and about, walking around, do you feel more attentive to what the world has to offer?

CMP: I shock myself with how colorful I am. Pre natural dyes, I was someone who wore a lot of black.... Now color, to me, is energy. When I see synthetic colors, it's not that I'm repulsed by them. I love a Day-Glo. But I feel much more soothed when I'm creating color from plants. You can get very vibrant, very acidic, and very poppy colors. And they all harmonize with one another in a way that I think synthetic color doesn't.

RJ: It's also the way that color has been made and used for thousands of years. It's an ancient process. Do you feel that sense of history behind you?

CMP: You're partaking in a craft that is as old as we are. Even in prehistory, there wouldn't have been another way to create color. I don't personally have an ancestral lineage to natural dyes. No one in my family's done it. When I first began, it almost felt like [I had] this slightly fraudulent complex, like, "Do I belong to this practice? Why am I so taken with this?" But I think it is that inherent knowledge that's within us, that it is connected to something that's part of our human history.

DIRECTORY:

Words:
Janis Jefferies

Textiles expert JANIS JEFFERIES on JEAN LURÇAT, the Frenchman who revived tapestry for the 20th century.

Jean Lurçat (1892–1966) believed tapestry was monumental art and should be experienced like a fresco. While well known for his paintings in the US in the 1920s, from the 1930s he dealt intensively with the form of picture carpets alongside his practice in engraving, poetry and ceramics.

In the years after the Second World War, Lurçat made a major contribution to the dying art of tapestry at a point when many large-scale, expensive European tapestry workshops had little economic viability and were losing money.[1] From his base among the centuries-old workshops of Aubusson, France, he introduced contemporary designs to tapestry, working directly on a full-scale cartoon (the name given to preparatory drawings in this medium) to lessen the number of steps from conception to completion. He simplified the weaving process by increasing the thickness of the wool used and by limiting the color palette. The success of Lurçat's tapestries inspired artists such as Joan Miró and Fernand Léger to take an interest in the possibilities of tapestry as an art form.

I first encountered Lurçat's tapestries when I was a student at London's Camberwell School of Arts and Crafts in 1974. His "Le Chant du Monde" (Song of the World) is a visionary sequence of 10 highly detailed tapestries woven between 1957 and 1966. They depict an entire cosmology of the ancient world as well as the dangers of that time—the terror of nuclear apocalypse—and offer hope that one day we may live in peace. Lurçat's use of narrative and text inspired me to make my own textile work about the Greenham Common Peace Camp, a women-led protest against nuclear weapons that took place at an airbase near London.

More recently, I had the privilege of hanging Lurçat's tapestries, including "Le Temps" (1958) at the first Triennial of Fiber Art in Hangzhou, China, in 2013. They were as stunning up close as I had imagined them to be from my studies.

Lurçat was also one of the founders of the International Centre for Ancient and Modern Tapestry (ICAMT) in Lausanne, Switzerland, which organized the International Tapestry Biennial from 1962 to 1995. So for more than 30 years, Lausanne was the capital of tapestry and textile art. Lurçat provided contemporary Western tapestry with a language of its own, influencing an entire generation of younger artists now known all over the world.

(1) Lurçat also brought a more contemporary aesthetic to the traditional world of tapestry. He was influenced by the Cubist innovations of Picasso and Braque but never followed them into the territory of pure abstraction. As Lurçat once put it: "To deprive a work of its subject is to deprive a sentence of its verb: meaning is lost, leaving the work devoid of all poetic impact."

OBJECT MATTERS

Words:
Stephanie d'Arc Taylor

Artwork: Falauke

A curious history of novelty objects.

What is a novelty item, anyway? Odds are you can name a few: a Magic 8 Ball from the possibility-rich post-WWII era, Chia Pets in the 1980s, the turn-of-the-millennium Big Mouth Billy Bass singing fish. But a definition is harder to come by. What do these objects have in common with each other? Why is it that, for a few short months, a pointless product can soar up the bestseller charts and then plummet like a stone?

Part of the appeal, surely, is the comfort that comes with participation in a collective. In 2000, during the first holiday season of the new millennium, seemingly every dad in the Western world felt the warm glow of community as they chortled along to Big Mouth Billy's tinny songs. President Bill Clinton reportedly gave one to his vice president, Al Gore. In *The Sopranos*, the dreams of mob boss (and dad) Tony Soprano are haunted by Big Mouth Billy Bass, as the toy was gifted to him by a traitorous friend he'd felt compelled to murder. Along with other novelty items that have become cultural touchstones—the pet rock, which made founder Gary Dahl a millionaire, and the plastic flamingo,

which now outnumbers its feathered doppelgängers—Big Mouth Billy Bass may be the physical actualization of a guffaw: a jolly, accessible joke that doesn't require much brainpower. Some might think him stupid, but he won't ever make *you* feel stupid.

For many of us, feeling in on the joke is worth a couple of bucks. But for the creators of lauded then discarded novelty items, the feeling lingers a lot longer—and can even go sour. Sometimes they even seem haunted by their roller-coaster success. Joe Pellettieri, the inventor of Big Mouth Billy Bass, insists, "I've had a lot of other hits that you may or may not be familiar with," before listing a few unfamiliar toys. Gary Dahl's feelings teeter into regret; in later years he wondered whether "life would have been simpler if I hadn't done it."

So before you toss your pet rock into the dust heap of history—or your Big Mouth Billy Bass into the landfill—spare a thought not just for their inventors, but for the trinkets that have soaked up so much derision in your home and in the culture. Punch lines get old, but the objects stick around.

LISA TADDEO

Words:
Jenna Mahale

On writing the secret lives of women.

If Lisa Taddeo gets stoned, she tends to reach for the same snack: "Grilled cheese is my number one," says the American author, who occasionally smokes marijuana to help "crack the code" of whatever she's working on at the time. Her method seems to be effective: Taddeo's work has earned her two Pushcart prizes, one British Book Award and, for her first book, *Three Women*, 11 weeks on *The New York Times* bestseller list. The nonfiction story—which is now being adapted into a TV series starring Shailene Woodley—was reported by Taddeo over eight years.[1] It follows three narratives: the affair an Indiana woman is conducting with her high school boyfriend; the sex life of a New England restaurateur whose husband has a cuckold fetish; and the perspective of Maggie, a North Dakotan who reflects on the relationship she had with her married English teacher as a high school student.

"For me, the line between fiction and nonfiction is an important one, but writing in and toward emotional truth is something I take with me into any form of writing that I do," says Taddeo, whose latest project is *Ghost Lover*, a collection of short stories. Here, she talks about empathy and perspective, the mysterious "you" that surfaces in her work, and the endless, fruitless search for quiet writing conditions in her home.

JENNA MAHALE: What's something you read recently that made you feel truly excited?

LISA TADDEO: *Luster* by Raven Leilani was the last thing that made me feel excited. I am a big fan of sentences, and her sentences are some of the best in modern literature.
JM: You often write in the second person, addressing an anonymous "you." Tell me a bit about how that mode is useful to you.

LT: When I used it in *Three Women* it was because I wanted people to be able to be pulled into Maggie's point of view and have to climb their way out so they could feel that before passing judgment. I personally like it because it really makes people think about what you're saying about another human being.
JM: *Three Women*, as well as this new collection of short stories, is made up of different women's voices and their separate narratives. What do you think is gained by overlapping those perspectives?

LT: Obviously I've spent a lot of time specifically with women and their stories, but I think this extends to everyone, really: The more we hear about other people who are not in our immediate circle, the more we are able to have empathy for one another. Even through something like social media, faces become human beings that we care about, with children, mothers and fathers, sisters and brothers.
JM: In an interview last year, you described your ideal writing environment as "Absolute quiet. No music, no birds, no pain, no joy." How do you go about achieving that?

LT: I mean, I haven't achieved it in a really long time. I've never written something good in a coffee shop even though I've tried to—I've wanted to be one of those people who did. Right now, I'm in our little office that's in an arts factory in Connecticut. And there's a woodworker downstairs who starts hammering things at noon. I'm constantly thinking about where I'm going to be left alone, and it's been almost impossible. I have a seven-year-old kid, so I cannot find quiet in my house. I used to do most of my writing late at night or very early in the morning, because I wasn't getting emails or phone calls then. But I've been too tired to work at night lately because of all the *Three Women* production work. So the answer to your question is: I don't know! I'm having a lot of trouble.
JM: You've said before that your interest in the subject of desire initially came from observing your parents' relationship. Is it funny to think your own daughter might one day feel the same way?

LT: What's funny is she doesn't like it when my husband and I show affection to each other. She's seven, so she's in this phase where she's like, "EW, YUCK!" whenever there's a boy kissing a girl on TV. I do give it a lot of thought, though. I remember being happy that my parents loved each other and were loving and affectionate with each other, but I was also grossed out. When I look back now that my parents have passed away, I feel like I wouldn't care what they did as long as they were here. But also [my husband and I] haven't had the time to be affectionate in front of her because we're just constantly working, so that's not been an issue. Yet.

(1) In the adaptation, Shailene Woodley will play Gia, a character based on Taddeo. Speaking to *Vanity Fair*, Taddeo explained that it made sense to incorporate herself as a character because her personality was central to getting the three women to talk openly. "I gave a lot of myself, and I was in a tough place, having lost much of my family, grieving and being alone. So these connections I made were more than a book for me," she said.

BAD IDEA: PAPER STRAWS

Words:
Ed Cumming

On the straw man of sustainability.

Plastic straws have long been portable reminders of the destruction we wreak on the environment. From roughly the 1960s until a couple of years ago—depending on where in the world you live—every take-out drink came with one. Some drinks, such as Capri Sun, included a tiny plastic straw as part of the product—one end cleaved to a sharp point with which to puncture the pouch. When finished, the straw was thrown away with the receptacle.

These straws—with a half-life of four million years—contributed to the more than eight million tons of plastic that enter Earth's waterways every year. They were ugly. They often came individually wrapped in paper, like tiny mouth syringes. More importantly for the fate of plastic straws, they were optional: For most people, a straw is not essential, it just makes drinking easier.

Companies looking to nod toward environmentalism without fundamentally changing their behavior saw plastic straws as a logical target for elimination. Paper equivalents seemed an obvious replacement. Metal straws were cold, expensive and heavy.

Paper straws retained the convenience, but they biodegraded, so you could toss them out without the same guilt that they would end up lodged within the stomach of an endangered animal.

Wrong. Paper straws are still carbon- and energy-intensive to produce, and several types are not even recyclable, unlike their plastic counterparts. This is ecological gesture politics, in which a tiny concession (straws make up 0.025% of ocean plastics) precludes more meaningful sacrifices, such as giving up driving, flying or eating meat.

There is also an acute problem with functionality.[1] After more than 10 seconds in liquid, the paper straw disintegrates. From pulp it came, and to pulp it returns. The drinker is left slurping harder and harder through the collapsed tube, which in turn speeds up the disintegration process. The drink begins to mix with mushy globules of cardboard. At last you give up, throw the damned thing away and drink from the cup. You curse the last straw. Perhaps that was the idea all along.

(1) Many disabled people criticize straw bans for not taking their needs into account. Paper straws often fall apart too quickly to be useful, particularly when used for hot beverages, and metal straws are inflexible. Although anyone may bring their own straw to a restaurant, it places the burden on the user to do so. As wheelchair user Alice Wong wrote for *Eater*: "Why would a disabled customer have to bring something in order to drink while non-disabled people have the convenience and ability to use what is provided for free? This is neither just, equitable, nor hospitable."

GOOD IDEA: LIFE STRAWS

Words: Harriet Fitch Little

Some straws offer users much more than mere convenience. In 2005, the Swiss company Vestergaard Frandsen released the Life Straw: a personal water purification device that filters out more than 99.99% of parasites and bacteria. What this means in real terms is that you might use one to suck water up from a muddy river, or from a toilet bowl (as one company boss did on a TV show), and that the water would come out crystal clear and potable. The life straw is a lifesaver, given that water-born pathogens cause more deaths every year than all forms of violence combined. Today, it is used in places where there is a chronic shortage of clean drinking water, in emergency zones (the company's first mass distribution was handing out 700,000 straws to victims of the 2005 earthquake in Kashmir), by off-grid adventurers and —increasingly—by households in affluent countries worried about the quality of tap water. These affluent buyers fund the organization's charity work, which centers on replicating the straw at scale so that whole communities can access safe water.

As the company told *Forbes* recently: "It's really a global public health company with a retail program."

ON BIRDWATCHING

Crossword: Mark Halpin

ACROSS

1. Danish shoe brand with global stores
5. Sir Guinness of film
9. Unsullied
13. Locale that's great for snorkeling
14. St. Petersburg's river
15. All over again
16. Tear to pieces
17. Repetitious, like the versions of a piece of writing
19. "Marsh bird forever!" as Irish birdwatchers would say?
21. "Mr. Blue Sky" band, for short
22. Actress Skye
23. Gathered into a pile
27. E.g., E. coli, for short
29. *Isle of Dogs* director Anderson
30. Airport screening group
31. Event for birdwatchers to mingle with some parrots?
35. Whittle (down)
36. Soldier or worker
37. Black, green, herbal, etc.
38. Medal for a birdwatcher who's spotted the second most passerine birds?
43. Take on a role
44. Chicken's preceder, perhaps
45. Some who 43 Across together
46. Oppressive authority, slangily personified
48. Woman's name that means "chaste"
50. Ryan of many a rom-com
53. Song in which a birdwatcher describes getting a bit too close to a sea bird?
56. Hans Christian Andersen offering
59. Riveting figure on a WWII poster
60. Lazily inert
61. Just scraped (out)
62. Merger

63. Epitome of goodness, metaphorically
64. Hardens
65. Religious group

DOWN
1. Musical merman
2. Back up someone's story
3. Goldfish in a Disney film
4. Mephistopheles, colloquially
5. Negatively charged particle
6. Leave alone
7. Always
8. Sticky confection
9. Ways of getting somewhere
10. Prefix with cycle or sex
11. Gun one's engine
12. Many a *Babe* character
13. Tennis legend Arthur
18. Audibly shocked
20. "I've _____ secret"
24. Busker's specialty
25. "To be," en español
26. Calendar components

28. Taiwanese tech giant
29. Dampens
31. Nab
32. Sour taste
33. Last part of a gerund
34. Off-roaders, for short
35. Exam for college-bound students, in brief
39. What you wouldn't want the boat you're in to be
40. Kindles
41. Decorated cupcakes, perhaps
42. Biblical late riser?
47. Bogged down
48. Archipelago component
49. Requires
51. "The Wasteland" poet Thomas Stearns
52. Secluded valley
54. Beverage commonly enjoyed with sushi
55. Vanished
56. Date relative
57. Kerfuffle
— —

CORRECTION: SPONTANEOUS GENERATION

Words:
Precious Adesina

A curious theory about the origins of life.

For centuries, people across the world believed that certain animals came from nonliving sources—a theory known as "spontaneous generation." Sacred documents from India remark on lice coming from sweat, Babylonian inscriptions mention that worms come from canal mud, the ancient Chinese thought that aphids came from bamboo, and other cultures believed that maggots were the product of rotting meat or that mice were created by soiled clothing mixed with wheat grains. Many Greek philosophers also believed that creatures appeared from lifeless matter whenever the conditions were right.

While today such a thought might seem ludicrous, it is easy to understand how people without recourse to modern science arrived at this point. It was hard to explain

why bread wrapped in cloth and put in a dark place might later be infested with mice. The organisms to which people applied the theory of spontaneous generation were often small enough that even sharp-eyed observers couldn't see them reproducing.

It took a surprisingly long time to debunk the theory. In the 1660s, Italian scientist and physician Francesco Redi placed one piece of fresh meat in an open container, another piece in a tightly covered jar, and one more in a jar covered in a porous material. Only the meat accessible to flies had maggots directly on it, and Redi concluded that maggots do not spontaneously arise from meat, but actually come from flies.

Redi's experiment didn't stop people from believing the apparent evidence of their own eyes, however, and the scientific tools of the Enlightenment were often turned toward proving rather than disproving spontaneous generation. In 1745, to demonstrate that microbes were spontaneously generated, English biologist and priest John Needham heated chicken broth (to kill any organism within it) before cooling it and placing the heated broth and an unheated one, as a control, in separate sealed containers. He was triumphant when he noted that both ended up with microbes in them. (In fact, this happened because the broth had been exposed to air after boiling, allowing microbes to get into it before the flask was sealed.)

The experiment that completely disproved the idea of spontaneous generation didn't come until the mid-19th century, when French chemist and microbiologist Louis Pasteur demonstrated that it wasn't the air that caused the microbes in the chicken broth.[1] Pasteur filtered out microorganisms while allowing air to pass through. His experiment confirmed that just because you couldn't see life, it didn't mean it wasn't there. This not only changed the course of what we now think about how living organisms come about but how germs should be treated, saving the lives of people even today.

(1) As late as 1877, *The New York Times* wrote that spontaneous generation was a debate where "both sides hold their own." The most prominent voice in favor of the theory at the time was that of Henry Charlton Bastian, a talented and well-respected disciple of Charles Darwin and pioneer of neurology, who believed that the principles of evolutionary biology led logically to support for the theory.

Photograph: *Dreaming Mantis* (2021) by David Brandon Geeting and Lina Sun Park.

LAST NIGHT

Words:
Rosalind Jana

What did jewelry designer SOPHIE BILLE BRAHE do with her evening?

Sophie Bille Brahe is a fine jewelry designer based in Copenhagen. Her celestial jewels often take inspiration from her ancestor Tycho Brahe, a renowned 16th-century astronomer who discovered a supernova in the Cassiopeia constellation.

ROSALIND JANA: Are you a night owl or an early bird?

SOPHIE BILLE BRAHE: I'm both. I enjoy the time I have by myself: late evening or early morning. But if I had to choose, I would be getting up early. . . . I had a little girl two years ago, but before her, my favorite time to work was five o'clock in the morning.

RJ: Do you have an evening routine?

SBB: I live close to the sea. When my kid is asleep, I go for a small evening walk with my dog. That's where I [sort out] all the thoughts that I didn't think through to the end during the day. After that walk, I have a feeling of calmness. Yesterday, when it had been raining, the lilacs smelled much stronger.

RJ: Are you someone who falls asleep easily?

SBB: Now, yes! But I don't need that much sleep. If I cannot sleep, I'm not stressing about it, I'm just relaxing. For me, the point between awake and asleep, a little bit like the point between sea and sky, is where I get all my ideas.

RJ: You're related to the astronomer Tycho Brahe. Are you interested in the night sky?

SBB: It's always been an overwhelming fascination. That's why I love diamonds. Even if they are from the ground, to me they are little stars. When I was a kid, my parents had a big terrace where we would stay out very late every summer. In August there are lots of shooting stars. We would try to sleep outside, but I remember in the early morning we would go [inside] to our parents' bed. But we tried!

RJ: Describe your perfect evening.

SBB: It would be with my best friends, maybe even my brother cooking. We are very close, and he's an amazing chef. We would sit in my garden when it was midsummer, and it doesn't really get dark. We'd stay up the whole evening, the whole night, and have a lovely dinner.

CULT ROOMS

Words:
Stephanie d'Arc Taylor

How California's empty swimming pools changed youth culture.

Los Angeles is a city that isn't meant to exist. Approaching the metropolis by land you pass through desert. It's dry, hot and arid. The only natural vegetation is that which clings to the sea-facing mountains, fed by mist that burns off as it travels inland. The water that feeds the palm trees and swimming pools—and which extinguishes the annual fires that the city is known for—is pumped hundreds of miles via the Mulholland Aqueduct, a scandalous piece of infrastructure that left a once-verdant valley to the northeast barren. Water—and drought—are as much a part of the story of Los Angeles as celluloid and freeways.

Endless summer, here, translates to endless drought. One drought in particular, which lasted from 1976 to 1977, was particularly momentous for American culture. At the same time as homeowners were unable to fill their swimming pools there was an innovation in skateboard wheel technology. Until

then, skateboarding had been a second-best sport for So-Cal surfers when the waves were flat. In the mid-'70s, skateboards were introduced with polyurethane wheels rather than clay or metal, which made skating nimbler, smoother and more forgiving.

A group of street kids from south Santa Monica and Venice, then down-and-out and known as Dogtown, seized the opportunity. Empty pools were a chance to go somewhere normally inaccessible; they were irresistible to the young and young at heart. The availability of these urban fantasylands, in combination with the novel skating technology, created a new form of youth culture.

Headquartered at the Zephyr skate shop on Main Street in Santa Monica, the self-appointed Z-boys—skaters like Tony Alva, Steve Olson, Stacy Peralta and Jay Adams—trawled the Westside of Los Angeles, searching for empty pools to ride. They were organized and industrious: When

they clocked a half-empty pool, they hauled over pumping equipment to finish the job. And when they were caught by an irate homeowner or the cops, they hauled ass on their decks, on to the next concrete wonderland.

The cant of the curving empty pool walls gave these skaters the momentum they needed to master astounding new tricks. When they competed in the Del Mar Nationals in 1975, the sport of skateboarding shook off its surfing roots and officially debuted under its own steam. Pool skating spread across the country, as far away as staid Cambridge, Massachusetts—where this photo was taken. The X Games, Jackass and blink-182 would follow, as would a documentary feature about the moment called *Dogtown and Z-Boys*.

The empty pool has been a site for other impish rogues including the English artist David Hockney, famous for his paintings

and printmaking collages of Southern California swimming pools.[1] Early one morning in 1988, he stole into the Hollywood Roosevelt hotel carrying spray cans and a broom. For four hours he worked at the bottom of the empty pool, creating a series of squiggles in blue within the basin. When filled with water, any disturbance would cause the squiggles to ripple to life.

The Roosevelt's management, needless to say, did not call the cops on the darling of the art world, busily adding a million dollars to the property value at the bottom of the empty pool. Ultimately, a special exemption was made to the state law requiring pool bottoms to be painted plain for safety. A soiree was held to celebrate the announcement. According to the *Los Angeles Times*, the pool was filled for the event. But no one went in. Despite the rippling squiggles, a pool restored with its rightful water just didn't have the same lure.

(1) The most famous of Hockney's paintings of swimming pools is *A Bigger Splash*, painted between April and June 1967. Speaking to Diane Hanson in 2009, he explained how the fixation began the first time he flew into LA: "I looked down to see blue swimming pools all over and I realized that a swimming pool in England would have been a luxury, whereas here they are not, because of the climate."

CREDITS:

COVER:	PHOTOGRAPHER	Romain Laprade
	STYLIST	Giulia Querenghi
	PRODUCER	Camila König
	HAIR & MAKEUP	Nika Ambrožič
	PHOTO ASSISTANT	Pol Masip Trullols
	MODEL	Aliou Gueye
	LOCATION	Ebro Delta, Spain

| ZAWE ASHTON | PHOTO ASSISTANT | Emilio Garfath |

| SPECIAL THANKS | | Ruth Kramer |
| | | Wildland |

STOCKISTS:
A — Z

A	ALEXANDER MCQUEEN	alexandermcqueen.com
	AN ONLY CHILD	anonlychild.com
	AURALEE	auralee.jp
B	BASERANGE	baserange.com
	BIANCA SAUNDERS	biancasaunders.com
C	CESAR	cesar.it
	CHARLOTTE CHESNAIS	charlottechesnais.com
D	DAVID CATALÁN	davidcatalan.store
	DEAR FRANCES	dearfrances.com
	DESALTO	desalto.it
E	ÉTUDES	etudes-studio.com
F	FRITZ HANSEN	fritzhansen.com
G	GALERIE CHENEL	galeriechenel.com
H	HERMÈS	hermes.com
	HOUSE OF FINN JUHL	finnjuhl.com
I	ISABEL MARANT	isabelmarant.com
	ISSEY MIYAKE	isseymiyake.com
J	JENNIFER FISHER	jenniferfisherjewelry.com
	JIL SANDER	jilsander.com
K	KENZO	kenzo.com
	KRUG	krug.com
M	MARSET	marset.com
	MOLLY GODDARD	mollygoddard.com
	MONSE	monse.com
	MYLO SWIM	myloswim.ca
O	OMEGA	omegawatches.com
	ONE&ONLY	oneandonlyresorts.com
	ORNAMENTUM GALLERY	ornamentumgallery.com
P	PARADE	yourparade.com
	PATOU	patou.com
	PAUL SMITH	paulsmith.com
	PETER DO	peterdo.net
	PRADA	prada.com
	PROENZA SCHOULER	proenzaschouler.com
R	RUI ZHOU	ruiofficial.me
S	SANDY LIANG	sandyliang.info
	SOPHIE BILLE BRAHE	sophiebillebrahe.com
	SNOW PEAK	snowpeak.com
	STRING FURNITURE	stringfurniture.com
T	TALLER MARMO	tallermarmo.com
	THE NEW CRAFTSMEN	thenewcraftsmen.com
	THEBE MAGUGU	thebemagugu.com
	TINA FREY	tf.design
	TOM FORD	tomford.com
V	VIPP	vipp.com
W	WILDLAND	wildland.scot
	WOLFORD	wolfordshop.com
Y	YAMAI	yamaijapan.com
Z	ZELL	zell.com.tr

MY FAVORITE THING

Words:
George Upton

GLADYS CHENEL, interviewed on page 86, on the Egyptian god that oversees her home.

We came across this sculpture of the Egyptian god Bes at a sale in America about 20 years ago. He's quite unusual. Bes was worshipped as the protector of the household and depictions of him are normally quite small. This one, however, was made by the Romans in the 1st century B.C.E. It's sculpted in nenfro, a kind of lava, which means it's surprisingly light and contrasts with his heavy, cartoonlike expression.

We had acquired the sculpture for our gallery but my husband and I came to fall in love with it. I was secretly quite happy when it didn't sell. Since then it has become part of the family. It's the piece that we have owned for the longest and the first object we find a home for when we have moved house. At the moment, it's in the dining room but in our last apartment it was in the hall. The children would play around him and we would dress him up when they had parties—we once gave him an eyepatch and tied a scarf around his neck when my son had a pirate-themed birthday.

He's really watched us grow up. It feels like we can talk to him, to tell him our secrets.